LEARNING THE EASY WAY

"He who learns not from history is destined to repeat it," says the familiar maxim. The Bible makes the same point regarding the Old Testament: "These things . . . were written down as warnings for us, on whom the fulfillment of the ages has come" (1 Cor. 10:11).

We face the same temptations and difficulties as the kings—and the ordinary people—of Israel faced: materialism, injustice, lesser gods, ritualized worship, basic selfishness. We can slide further and further into disobedience until we plunge over the edge of judgment, or we can listen to men such as Elijah, Amos, and Jeremiah (and their modern counterparts) and do what is "right in the eyes of the Lord" (2 Kings 22:2).

The choice is ours.

Other *BIBLE ALIVE* titles:

OLD TESTAMENT SURVEYS
    Let Day Begin
    Freedom Road
    Years of Darkness, Days of Glory
    Lift High the Torch
    Springtime Coming

NEW TESTAMENT SURVEYS
    The Servant King
    The Great Adventure
    Regions Beyond
    Christ Preeminent
    Pass It On
    His Glory

LARRY RICHARDS
BIBLE ALIVE SERIES

Edge of Judgment

Pathways to Blessing. . .and Judgment

Studies in I and II Kings, II Chronicles, prophets
of the Divided and Surviving Kingdoms,
Ezekiel, and Jeremiah

4549

David C. Cook Publishing Co.
ELGIN, ILLINOIS—WESTON, ONTARIO
LA HABRA, CALIFORNIA

EDGE OF JUDGMENT
© 1977 David C. Cook Publishing Co.

Published by David C. Cook Publishing Co.,
850 N. Grove Ave., Elgin, IL 60120
Printed in the United States of America

ISBN 0-89191-060-3

CONTENTS

EDGE OF JUDGMENT

THE JOURNEY

HABAKKUK TOILED SLOWLY ALONG THE ROAD, angling toward the sun, which would soon disappear into the Mediterranean beyond the mountains of Ephraim. He moved steadily, head bent, eyes downcast, unmindful of the crunch of his sandals on the gravel or the swish of his long cloak.

Habakkuk was clearly a Hebrew, with strong, heavy features. He wore his hair long, and over it a large square of linen was folded triangularly and tied with a cord knotted beneath his beard. His large, shapeless cloak looked something like a Roman toga. Unlike the cloaks of most Jews of his day, which were made of heavy woolen cloth, his was of linen. Of course, it was Palestinian linen, and not the fine linen of Egypt he wore when singing before the Lord in the Temple. Nevertheless, the possession of linen marked Habakkuk as a man of means.

It was also apparent that Habakkuk was a man

with a burden. Every now and then he would stop, look up toward the heavens, and seem to sigh. Then, with head slumping even lower on his chest, he would trudge on.

To most, it would seem that this twenty-first year of the reign of the godly king Josiah should be a time of joy for any worshiper of Jehovah—especially for a Levite, devoted to God's service. Not many years before, all Judah had worshiped idols. King Manasseh had even erected a carved god in the house of the Lord itself. But now Josiah ruled, and Josiah had a heart for the living God (2 Kings 22: 1, 2).

Josiah had come to the throne of Judah at the age of eight. As a youth of sixteen, he had begun to seek after God. When Josiah was only twenty, he had purged idolatry from Jerusalem and traveled as far as Naphtali to destroy centers of heathen worship in his land. Josiah ground the idols into dust, desecrated their unholy places with the bones of the dead, and destroyed the false priests who stole men's hearts away from Israel's God. King Josiah also restored Temple worship in Jerusalem to its central place in the religious life of the nation and regathered the priests and Levites to minister there.

And so, just nine years before, Habakkuk himself had left his hometown of Shechem to come to render the sacrifice of praise, offered on the strings of his instrument and on his lips, moved by a deep sense of the glory and goodness of God.

The next years had been happy ones. Busy ones. The service of God was organized, the singers drilled and trained, the old psalms of David fitted

10

again to the worship for which they had been designed. The high point had been reached when, after six full years of preparation, the massive task of repairing and refurbishing the Temple was begun. This work had unexpectedly led to the discovery that gave Habakkuk his greatest joy in life—and which was now the cause of his torment.

In the process of extensive repair, Hilkiah the priest had discovered a copy of the Book of the Law—that book which God had given Israel through Moses. Tradition said such a book existed. But it had been lost so long that none of Habakkuk's generation had seen it or could say with certainty what it might contain. Shaphan, the scribe, read the book, then hurried to Jerusalem. King Josiah must hear what this book had to say! (2 Kings 22:11)

The book made a tremendous impact on the king. It contained not only the history of the nation's call by God, but also the explicit instructions of God given at Sinai. At the very end of the lost books of Moses in the section that today is called Deuteronomy, was recorded the curse of God outlining what would happen should Israel forsake God's Law.

The king and his countrymen were stricken with terror. No one then living could remember a day when Judah had known and obeyed the commands they found in this book! Immediately, Josiah humbled himself before God and prayed for mercy. He determined to publish the divine Law throughout his realm. As king, Josiah made a solemn promise to Jehovah to keep His commands and His statutes

11

with all his heart and soul.

Publish God's Word, Josiah did. He required everyone to hear the Book read, and that very year, he reinstituted the Feast of Passover. Josiah led all Judah to keep it with great rejoicing (2 Kings 23:21,22).

It was in this—in knowing and doing the Law of God—that Habakkuk, too, found his greatest joy, just as had the psalmist David whose words Habakkuk now sang in a restored Temple.

> I rejoice at thy word,
> as one that findeth great spoil. . . .
> My soul hath kept thy testimonies;
> and I love them exceedingly.
> *Psalm 119:162, 167 (KJV)*

But it was also here, in the Law of God, that Habakkuk found his present torment.

While Habakkuk loved his people and his nation, his overwhelming passion was for the Lord. As part of the Temple community, Habakkuk had many opportunities to hear the Word of God as it was read and discussed. Each word told Habakkuk more of his God, and the more he heard the more exalted God, the Holy One, became in Habakkuk's eyes. As Habakkuk began to see the perfect holiness of God, he became more and more concerned about the imperfections and sins of God's people. True, idolatry was gone, and men now worshiped Jehovah. Josiah was working tirelessly to promote knowledge of the Law in his kingdom. But it was also clear that the religious reformation was superficial. The hearts of the men and women who came to worship at the Temple in Jerusalem were the same as when they had worshiped at pagan altars!

A knowledge of the Law did not automatically produce holiness, and God's sinning people were not obeying the commands of their God.

To Habakkuk, the situation was intolerable. Here was Judah, a people called by the name of God, blessed with the Law of God, daily bringing shame on His holy name by flagrant disregard of that Law, by perversion of its holy standards, and by violence against those who would try to walk by it!

This was Habakkuk's burden as he left Jerusalem and the Temple and trudged up the mountain road toward his home. He must think through the reasons why his constant prayer for revival went unanswered. And such is the complaint on Habakkuk's lips now, as he stops, his arms half raised, gazing questioningly toward the heavens.

O Jehovah! How long must I cry for help,
  and you not respond?
I cry to you of violence, yet you do not deliver.
Why do you make me constantly gaze on wicked-
    ness?
    you yourself endure the sight of mistreat-
      ment?
Havoc and violence are before me,
  causing strife and contention to arise.
In this situation law is benumbed,
  justice ever absent,

13

for with the wicked overwhelming the righteous
  perverted justice is administered.

Habakkuk 1:2-4*

This condition of violence and perverted justice is difficult for us to understand today. Why, if the king was righteous, was law benumbed and justice ever absent? The answer is found in the way law was administered in the Judah of Habakkuk's day.

While the king's power may have been supreme in Jerusalem, where he reigned through his personal officers, outside the capital the administration of justice was a local affair. There was no code of statutory law administered by trained officials and enforced by public police. Cases were brought by individuals before local justices who sat at the city's gates. The plaintiff and defendant each brought witnesses to give evidence, and each pled his own case.

There were many ways that such justice could be perverted. False witnesses were easy to hire in Judah. Or a friendly lie might be told for a neighbor in return for the promise of similar help later. And the men who made the decisions were not above a bribe; many went out of their way to seek them. By sheer weight of numbers those who tried to keep the law and do justice might be overwhelmed and defrauded by the wicked around them. Justice was

* The translation of Habakkuk is the author's paraphrase from the Hebrew text.

14

administered, but it was a perverted and crooked sort of justice.

The passionate words of Isaiah, who looked at a "religious" people much like those of Habakkuk's day, echo what must often have troubled Habakkuk's thoughts.

> To what purpose is the multitude of your sacrifices unto me? saith the Lord. I am full of the burnt-offerings of rams, and the fat of fed beasts: and I delight not in the blood of bullocks, or of lambs, or of the goats. When ye come to appear before me, who hath required this at your hand, to tread my courts? Bring no more vain oblations; incense is an abomination to me; the new moons and sabbaths, the calling of assemblies, I cannot away with; it is iniquity, even the solemn meeting. Your new moons and your appointed feasts my soul hateth; they are a trouble onto me: I am weary to bear them. And when ye spread forth your hands, I will hide mine eyes from you: yea, when ye make many prayers I will not hear: your hands are full of blood. Wash you, make you clean, put away the evil of your doings from before mine eyes; cease to do evil; learn to do well; seek judgment, relieve the oppressed, judge the fatherless, plead for the widow.
>
> *Isaiah 1:11-17 (KJV)*

Now Habakkuk's thoughts lay not so much with the people as with God. He was not so moved by anger as by concern for the glory of the Lord. How could a holy God let His people go on like this and dishonor Him? Must not God move to remedy the situation? Must He not move the hearts of the people as He had moved Josiah's, and bring Judah to love and obey Him? Must not God be glorified in the sight of all the heathen?

The way was long. Now falling shadows began to obscure the pathway. The chill of the Judean hills slipped beneath Habakkuk's cloak and woke him to the need to hurry. These were deep thoughts. Thoughts that needed to be pondered. But this was not the time or the place.

Wrapping his cloak about him, Habakkuk lengthened his stride and hurried on.

BACKGROUND

In the vast world of the East, Palestine lay as an insignificant shadow on the western borders of the colossal Assyrian Empire. For over a century this pulsing collection of tribes and peoples had been held together by force, violently wielded by a series of strong rulers. Periodic rebellions within, pressures from the Indo-European peoples on her northern borders, and incursions of Arab tribes in eastern Palestine and Syria kept the colossus in constant turmoil. Men like Ashurbanipal, who ruled Assyria until 633 B.C., had been able to contain these surging forces. But the two rulers who succeeded him, Assuretililani and Sinsharishkun, proved far too weak. The weakening was felt in Palestine, which had been a tributary of Assyria, and partially ex-

16

plains how Josiah was able to take such strong measures in destroying worshipers of both Canaanite and Assyrian gods and in strengthening his kingdom. With Assyria engaged on so many fronts, there was no immediate danger of vengeance.

Judah was used to living on the edge of judgment. Following the glory days of the Davidic and Solomonic Kingdom, the nation had been divided into two kingdoms. The northern section, which kept the name Israel, had an unbroken series of godless kings. Finally, God acted in judgment, and in 722 B.C., Sargon II destroyed the northern nation, carried away the people into captivity, and resettled a scattering of pagan people on Israel's ancient land.

The deportation of Israel had been a warning to Judah. God would not wink at sin. Many prophets had warned the Northern Kingdom and had been ignored or persecuted. Many prophets had spoken out in warning to Judah. Yet neither the prophets' ministry nor the object lesson of Israel's deportation had convinced the Southern Kingdom or brought wholehearted repentance.

Unlike the divided Israel, Judah had several godly kings who attempted to lead the nation back to God. Some impact had been made, as by Josiah. Yet the underlying trend was downward. Reforms were superficial; the hearts of people remained untouched. Even constant danger from great world powers surrounding them failed to move God's people to turn to Him.

The history of the Southern Kingdom is the history of a people who chose to walk ever closer to

17

judgment, and of the prophetic messengers God sent to warn them back to His safe pathways.

Now, in Habakkuk's day, the end was drawing rapidly near. The unhappy Levite, deeply concerned for both his nation and his God, was about to become the bearer of news of the fast-approaching day of darkness.

In Judah, everyone was sure that the danger from Assyria has lessened. Even the troubled Habakkuk, resting on his mat in his home in Shechem, could not be aware of what was happening in the faraway city of Babylon.

In 626 B.C., just five years before Habakkuk began his lonely journey, Nabopolassar, a Chaldean prince, led a rebellion and defeated the Assyrians outside the city of Babylon. He took the city and the throne and established the Neo-Babylonian Empire. The Assyrians repeatedly tried to dislodge him, but fighting fiercely on the defensive, Nabopolassar maintained his hold on the city. Even had Habakkuk been informed of the situation in far-off Babylon, he could hardly have foreseen the developments that less than two decades would bring.

By 620, Nabopolassar would form an alliance with the Medes, a fierce people on Assyria's northeastern border. This coalition would make great inroads in Assyrian territory. Soon Assyria would be fighting for her very life. Within five years of Habakkuk's journey, Egypt, Assyrian's ancient enemy, would see such danger from the Medeo-Babylonian axis that she even would send an army to Assyria's support!

Just two years after that, in 614 B.C., the Medes

took the ancient capital of Asshur. By 612, the allies assaulted Nineveh, the impregnable citadel of Assyria, and destroyed it within three months. This was the death of Assyria. It was now merely a matter of time before the terror that the name of Assyria had raised in the hearts of generations of Hebrews would be transferred to the name of Babylon. Within another fifteen years, Nebuchadnezzar, Nabopolassar's greater son, would begin a series of deportations that by 589 B.C. would leave the Temple a smoking, crumbling ruin.

All this Habakkuk could not know. But Habakkuk's God *did* know, and as His exhausted servant tossed that night on his straw mat, wrapped in a woolen cloak like the linen one he had worn during the day, God spoke to the man who was so concerned with His glory. God revealed to him the instrument He was even then preparing, which could chastise His sinning people and bring them, through fiery judgment, to the place of obedience and revival.

> Look among the nations—consider,
>   and be dumb with astonishment.
> For there is a work I am performing in your
>   days
>   that you will never begin to believe when it is
>   revealed.
> For see!
>   I am raising up the Chaldeans;
>   that fierce and rapacious people,
>   who plunder throughout the breadth

of the earth to take possession of dwellings
   not their own.
A terrible, dreadful people, this:
   Imposing its own judgment and authority.
Its horses are swifter than leopards,
   keener than evening wolves,
   its horsemen spring.
It derides kings;
   princes, to it, are objects of derision.
It laughs at every fortification,
   then proceeds to heap up dirt and take it.
Then it shall pass on, a wind,
   and proceed to sweep over you and trans-
     gress.
This, its power, is its god.

Habakkuk 1:5-11

Habakkuk started from his sleep, eyes searching through the thatched bows of the arbor on the roof where he slept. He could see no shape. Stare as he could, only the cold stars far above looked back at him through the darkness. Suddenly he was aware of tension, as the muscles of his legs, unused to such a journey as he had traveled the day before, bunched and cramped. Habakkuk fell back on his pallet, forced himself to relax. He was no mystic, and he had sought no vision. Yet Habakkuk recognized the voice he had heard, and the indelible mark of authority that rested on each syllable of the message. Had he been awake or asleep? Had God spoken *to* him, or *in* him? He did not know. But he did know God had spoken. And the message of God was a

20

vivid warning of judgment!

The men of the East were well acquainted with conquest, and the meaning of the foretold invasion was clear to Habakkuk. His thoughts turned to the hoards of men who would overrun the countryside, pillaging, stripping it of everything edible.

He knew the fate awaiting those who locked themselves in fortified cities. No matter how massive the walls, how clever the castellated design of the defense towers, how large the supply of food, the attacking army was well able to isolate each city and well equipped with siege engines to batter and take it. A steep embankment of earth and rubble would be quickly thrown up against the wall, and battering rams would pound against its base. Or a pit might be dug against the foundations of the wall, and a fire built there. The soft limestone, which had little resistance to heat, would crumble in a useless heap.

And when the city was finally taken by assault, the horrors awaiting its inhabitants were indescribable. The fortunate were taken into captivity, to face death in slavery. Others, brought in chains and cages to the conquering monarch, were tortured and blinded or burned alive for his entertainment, then tossed aside into heaps of writhing agony.

All this, Jehovah said, was coming, straining and hastening toward Judah. And all this, Jehovah said, was His work. He was raising up the Chaldeans, and He was riding at the head of the dreadful scourge.

To Habakkuk, who understood the holiness of God and who saw beneath the facade of Judah's apparent reform its continuing depravity, there

could be no doubt about justice. And no retreat to a
fuzzy concept of love that robs God of His holiness
and leaves Him the emasculated image honored by
the wishful thinkers of all ages. Habakkuk knew
God's love for the people He had chosen. And
Habakkuk knew the cancer that now infected the
body of Jehovah's beloved.

The cancer of sin had led to Habakkuk's original
cry. The surgery the divine Physician decreed could
warrant no recrimination. No, Habakkuk looked
into the face of God and saw His unchanging purpose and love now expressed as chastisement.

> Aren't you Jehovah of old?
> My God? My Holy One?
> We shall not perish.
> Jehovah, you have appointed it as a judgment;
> O Rock, you have ordained it as a correction.
> *Habakkuk 1:12*

Now the Levite's thoughts had drifted back to
God. Judgment must come, but God was unchanging. His love for His people would never wane.

The same stars that looked down on Habakkuk
had witnessed the covenant God made with
Abraham more than a millennium before. They
could testify to God's faithfulness, for they had seen
Moses lead the nation out of Egypt and observed
Joshua's victories. The stars that symbolized the un-
counted strength of Abraham's seed had seen Israel
slip into apostasy and gross idolatry. They had
watched as a weakened, puny people were restored

and raised to glory by David, the worshiping warrior whose songs of praise Habakkuk himself echoed four hundred years later.

No. We shall not perish. For you are Jehovah of old.

With these thoughts of God, came rest. Soon the weary body relaxed, the tired eyes closed, and the bearded mouth twitched into a smile. Habakkuk was asleep.

GOING DEEPER

The following study suggestions are provided to help you explore the Bible itself and its meaning for you.

to personalize

1. The Old Testament prophets were men like us, who spoke out of a definite historical situation. Looking over the first chapter of Habakkuk and the following historical references,

   a. How would you describe Habakkuk the man?

   b. How would you describe the historical setting in which he spoke?

   c. How would you describe the message God seems to be delivering through him?

   References to study: Hab. 1; 2 Chron. 33—35; 2 Kings 22: 1—23: 30.

2. From what you've seen thus far, how important do you think knowing the historical situation is in understanding the ministry and messages of the Old Testament prophets?

3. If God were to speak through a prophet today,

what message do you think He would stress? Why?

4. Habakkuk seems to speak out of a deep sense of who God is, and to anchor his interpretation even of this message of judgment in assurance that God is a trustworthy and loving Person.

Here are several passages from the books Josiah discovered that might give a basis for that confidence: Gen. 15:1-21; Exod. 15:1-18; Deut. 11.

5. From the three passages you explored in 4 (above), what is *your* picture of God? How do you respond when He disciplines you?

to probe
First read the following description:

Karen is a single woman who now works for a Christian organization. She has overcome many of her earlier feelings of failure and inadequacy but still becomes despondent quite often. Usually when things go wrong, she becomes upset with God, sometimes even describing her reaction as "livid with anger." Later she feels ashamed and realizes her feelings are inappropriate. But life is often hard for her, and she does respond rebelliously when discipline comes.

How much of Karen's reaction do you believe comes from a faulty image of God? What do you think Karen's inner image of God really is—what does she feel deep-down that He is like? How did Habakkuk see God? How much of a person's response to situations in life depend on how he or she views God?

Write down your ideas on this in a four- to five-page paper.

2

Habakkuk 1:13–3:19

THE PINNACLE

SHECHEM, THE ANCIENT LEVITICAL CITY from which Habakkuk came, lay in a protected pass between the two mountains of Ebal and Gerizim. Habakkuk knew these mountains well. He had played over them as a boy. Awakened now by the bright sun, Habakkuk breathed the air of his boyhood home and looked out over a familiar scene.

On a visit home all men seem to find lost appetite, and Habakkuk was no exception. From the house below he smelled the bread his sister was preparing. She had risen early to grind the coarse barley meal that, mixed with salt and water and formed into flat cakes, was the staple food of the Hebrews. With the cakes, Habakkuk knew, would be soured goat's milk, relished as a thirst quencher, and perhaps a cake of dried figs. The Hebrews did not eat heavily in the morning: their large meal was reserved for evening. But this was a special occasion, and Habakkuk was hungry.

25

After the meal, during which he said nothing of the occurrence of the night, he took two lightly roasted ears of corn and, over the protests of the family, headed alone up toward the heights of Mount Ebal. On the way, Habakkuk reviewed the revelation of the night and, as he considered it, his face once again tightened into a frown. God had solved the problem of Judah's sin. Habakkuk saw the logic and purpose of God in bringing judgment on His people. But what about this instrument God was raising up to use? Didn't God's use of the Chaldeans have far-reaching implications?

Habakkuk's reasoning started with God. He knew God was holy, and that therefore He could not endure wickedness. Then how could God endure the wickedness of Chaldea? Surely the Babylonians in their mad cause would overrun nations more righteous than they. In the judgment on the wicked of Judah, would the righteous escape? Seeing the rampaging Chaldeans sweep over nation after nation, ravaging them at will, what would men think of the God who allowed this? And what idea of God would the Chaldeans have? It seemed clear to Habakkuk that the Chaldeans would conclude that there is no sovereign God ruling mankind. Men must seem to them to be like fish, with only the skill of the fisherman limiting the catch. The Chaldean's success would lead him to make his own power his god! Such boasting would dishonor the true God, who alone permitted the Chaldeans to prosper and worked out His purpose through them.

As these thoughts swirled, the conviction grew

that Habakkuk now faced an even greater problem
than the one that had troubled him at first:

> You are too pure of eye to be a witness to evil,
>> are not able to endure the sight of mistreat-
>> ment.
> Why then do you endure the sight of the
>> treacherous?
>> keep silent when the wicked engulfs
>> one more righteous than he?
> Yet you have made men like fishes of the sea!
>>> like a creeping thing,
>> in that there is no one ruling over him.
> He brings all of them up with hooks,
>> he is accustomed to collect them in his seine,
>>> to gather them in his dip net.
> So he sacrifices to his seine,
>> and makes burnt offerings to his dip net,
>> for through them his portion is rich,
>>> and his food fat.
> Will he then keep on emptying out his seine,
>> and continue to destroy nations without
>> compassion?
>
> *Habakkuk 1:13-17*

Surely the God who had spoken earlier to His
troubled servant would speak again. Habakkuk
looked around, aware again of his surroundings. He
was on a familiar trail. From the top of Ebal he
would soon look off to the north and west and see
the spot where Samaria had rested proudly on her
magnificent hill. There, on the top of Ebal, where

once had been a watchtower, where once signal fires, the telegraph of the ancient Near East, were lit—there Habakkuk would wait.

> I will watch—
>   stand on the watch tower—
> and look to see what He will say in me,
> and how I can answer my reasoning.
> *Habakkuk 2:1*

Habakkuk climbed. Climbed to the top. And there on the ancient watchtower Habakkuk took his stand . . . to wait.

MONOLOGUE

The message of a coming Chaldean invasion was not new. God's prophet had foretold such a captivity (Isa. 39), and that word would surely be fulfilled. Someday. But the startling thing about the revelation of the night was that God's day of judgment had now come! There, in Habakkuk's watchtower, with the hot sun pounding into his shoulders, the message of immediacy was repeated.

> Then Jehovah responded:
> Write the vision;
>   make it so plain on the signboards
>   that a running man can read it.
> For the vision has a yet future appointment—
>   it pants for fulfillment
>   and is no lie.

28

Though it delay, wait for it. . .
For it most surely is coming
and will not be late.

Habakkuk 2:2, 3

With this command to publish God's sentence of judgment given, the Lord addressed Himself to Habakkuk's private problem. God showed him, and us, why it is that the course the wicked run in their vain attempt at self-glorification can never tarnish the glory of God.

First God commanded Habakkuk to look at the character of the wicked man. He suffers from a fatal flaw that drives him on, seeking a satisfaction he can never find. Like the sinner of every age, the Chaldean's pride and conquest would only feed the furnace of his desire. As passion is enflamed, the emptiness within is enlarged, and he is driven to push further on into sin in his vain attempt to find satisfaction.

How different for the man of God, who seeks only the will of God, and finds in God a peace and joy that satisfies! The Chaldean has taken a course that leads only to self-enslavement and to frustration, for there is no peace for man but in God.

Look! He is swelled with pride,
His inmost soul is perverted.
(But the righteous man will live by his faith.)
Indeed, this wine is heady
The haughty hero will never be at rest:
He who has magnified himself

29

is like hell—
he is like death—
He will never be satisfied.
He will keep on gathering all the nations
keep on assembling all the peoples
to himself.

Habakkuk 2:4, 5

No, Habakkuk, there is no turning back from this course. And look where it leads! Not only does the Chaldean find no satisfaction, he earns repayment! The people of the conquered nations have a proverb: "Your turn will come!"

Won't all those certainly apply a proverb to
him?
a taunting truism that is a riddle to him?
and say
"Woe to the man who adds to that which is not
his!
How long? He is weighing himself down with
heavy debts."
Won't those that owe you interest suddenly
arise,
those awake who will shake you with violence,
and you (in turn) be a spoil for them?
Because you yourself plundered many nations,
all the rest will plunder you.
This because of bloodshed—
the violence done the land,
the city,
and all her inhabitants.

Habakkuk 2:6-8

30

God continues now to point out that men such as the Chaldean seek security. They think wealth and power protect them. Instead, the results of such a life-style is dashed hopes and guilt.

> Woe to the man who is reaping dishonest revenues for his household,
>> to build with security,
>> to deliver himself from the power of calamity.
> You have really advised only dashed hopes for your household,
>> destruction for many peoples,
>> and in the process are gaining
>> only guilt for your soul.
> A stone (of such a structure) will cry out of a wall,
> and a rafter out of the timbers answers it.
>> *Habakkuk 2:9-11*

And what will happen to those who pile up and build material things? What of the wealth assemblied; the palaces and cities constructed? Like Samaria once proud and beautiful and built on blood, all will become ruins. What a judgment that the builders build for nothing! God's earth is destined to be filled with the knowledge of the Lord, not with monuments of murderers!

> Woe to the one who builds a city in blood,
>> and establishes it on injustice.
> Look! Isn't it (a judgment) from Jehovah
>> that the peoples toil only to satisfy fire?

31

> that people go on piling up profits—
>> for nothing?
> For the earth is destined to be filled
> with the knowledge of Jehovah;
>> as the waters blanket the seas.
>
> *Habakkuk 2:12-14*

So also do all man's plots to promote himself at the expense of others lead to appropriate judgments.

> Woe to the one who gets his neighbor to drink,
>> to you who mix drinks with hidden malice.
> Yes, you get him drunk,
>> to gaze on him in the gutter!
> It will come round to you, the cup of Jehovah's
>> right hand.
> Then vomit will pollute your glory,
>> for the violence done to Lebanon,
>>> and the devastation of the wild beasts
>>> that terrify them will cover you!
> This because of bloodshed—
>> the violence done the land,
>>> the city,
>>>> and all her inhabitants.
>
> *Habakkuk 2:15-17*

Habakkuk has feared for God's glory, concerned at the success of the sinner. He has worried that puny men will exalt themselves and boast of victory over God. Yet *every sinful act brings its own judgment within the sinners' personalities and in circumstances as well!* No need to fear for God! The idols of men of every age are empty things.

What good has an idol ever been,
   that the idolater should carve it?
   or the image and its false priest,
     that the idolater should trust in it?
      to create dumb gods!
Woe to the man who says to a stick of wood,
   "Wake up!"
   "Awake!" to silent stone.
Do you expect it to teach?
Look, it is encased in gold and silver,
   but there is nothing of breath inside.
But Jehovah is in His holy temple:
Be silent before Him, entire world.

Habakkuk 2:18-20

The idols of men, whether of wood and stone or of wealth and success, hold no hope. God is in His Holy Temple. God is Judge. And God is about to judge!

JUDGMENT

The divine monologue satisfied Habakkuk's concern for God's honor. He began to realize that the wicked men of every age make choices which guarantee their misery. The man who seeks a million dollars at the expense of others may gain it—but reaching the goal will never satisfy him. Instead it will enlarge his desire for more. He will be driven on, ever seeking but never finding the satisfaction he yearns for.

And the very actions he takes to reach his goal will

ultimately trip him up: the enemies he makes and the men and women he harms will one day treat him as he has treated them.

God's judgment does not wait on eternity; God's judgment is exercised now, in the emptiness, insecurity, and anxiety even "successful" sin brings.

Reassured that God's holiness has been protected, Habakkuk responds to the words spoken to him.

> Jehovah,
> I have heard your message:
> I fear, Jehovah.
>> Call your work to life soon,
>>> soon make it known.
>> In wrath you will remember mercy.
>>>> *Habakkuk 3:2*

Habakkuk's prayer reveals a fear at the prospect of judgment on Judah but also a great yearning for the purifying work to take place. After all, Habakkuk thinks, in wrath God will surely remember mercy! It can't be *too* bad.

Satisfied, Habakkuk is ready now to leave the pinnacle where he has waited for God's answer; but God is not ready to release him. Habakkuk must yet be brought to another peak: the pinnacle of faith.

The sun is drifting now just a few feet above the horizon. Habakkuk has been standing all day as Jehovah reasoned with him, explaining the principles of judgment that continually operate in man's world. Now, when Habakkuk turns to leave, his body will not move! He tries to drop his arms, but they are fixed, raised toward the heavens. His staring eyes are fixed on the setting sun. And, gently as a shadow, the voice of God seems to drift across his thoughts. "Ah, child, you pray for judgment? Do you know what judgment means?"

Quietly, naturally, Habakkuk's mind slips back to the Word of God and to the history of his people. Yes, Israel has known judgment. Israel has often felt the chastening hand of God. Habakkuk remembers Israel at Kadesh, a story he has often heard from the book we call Numbers. *And suddenly, it seems Habakkuk is there!*

Habakkuk sees the sinning people as they cry out against the Lord who has brought them out of Egypt. As their rebellion and ingratitude grow, Habakkuk sees the hills of Teman and Paran suddenly begin to glow. There, along the pathway the people of Israel have taken from Sinai, a phosphorescent brilliance is moving toward them, lighting up the land for miles around. As Habakkuk watches, his very soul quakes. He realizes that this vision is the Holy One of Israel, the God who gave His Law on Sinai, moving out in righteous wrath to judge.

> God began to come from Teman,
>   the Holy One from the mountains of Paran.
>   Consider!
> His splendor covers the heavens
> His glory fills the earth
> His brightness flashes like sunlight
> Blinding brilliance shimmers at His hands,

only concealing His elemental power!
Plague precedes Him
Burning pestilence marks His footsteps
He stands; examines a land . . .
    primeval mountains shatter
    ancient hills crumble
(Such) His majestic march of old!
Habakkuk 3:3-6

And then the vista changes. Now Habakkuk sees the tents of Israel spread across the land of Midian. He sees the whoredom Israel committed with the Moabites, embracing their daughters and their gods. And Habakkuk sees the chastening plague from God sweep through the camp, the writhing agony of those who feel the fury of a God determined to save—and willing to save through punishment.

I saw the tents pitched in Cushan under terror,
The shaking of tent doors in the land of Midian,
    Was it against the rivers, Jehovah?
    Did your anger rage against rivers
      or your fury burst on the seas?
    that you should mount your horses
      your chariots of salvation?
Your bow is unslung,
    Chastisements' oath sworn.
      Consider.
Habakkuk 3:7-9

And then a flashing panorama of God's cataclys-

mic judgments rips like thunderbolts before
Habakkuk's seared eyes.

You split open the earth—formed rivers—
Mountains saw you—they writhed.
Floods of waters swept over;
The subterranean waters roared,
lurched their strength high.
Sun, moon froze in the heights
as light from your arrows shot by,
the shine of your flashing spear.

Habakkuk 3:9-11

And through it all, one fact fastens firmly in
Habakkuk's mind. For God's people, the judgments
are purifying. The nations might be destroyed. But
not Israel.

Then, in his ultimate role of Judge, God steps
from His throne to mount His great war chariot and
bring destruction on those who afflict His people.

It was in indignation you trod the land,
how much more the nations!
You came out to save your people
to deliver your anointed.
You severed the head of the house of the
wicked,
you lay bare the base of his neck.
Consider!
You split the heads of the storming hoards
with their own spears
those who storm along to scatter me
who rejoice to devour the poor in secret,

37

> You tread the seas,
>> your horses the great foaming waters.
>>> *Habakkuk 3:12-15*

The vision over, Habakkuk crumples to the ground. He struggles to rise, fully conscious. But where his limbs have been stiff and fixed, they now tremble, limp and useless. Habakkuk, who had prayed lightly for judgment to come quickly, now knew what judgment would mean. For Habakkuk had seen God the Judge.

> I heard
>> then my inmost soul shook;
>> at the voice my lips quivered,
>> rottenness began to dissolve my bones,
>> my knees shook
>>> that I was to wait quietly for the day of
>>>> distress,
>>> for the attacker to invade the nation.
>> The fig tree will not blossom,
>> There will be no yield from the vines.
>> The olive will fail,
>> The fields not bear grain.
>> The flock be cut off from the fields,
>> No cattle in the stall.
>>> *Habakkuk 3:16–18*

And this judgment was coming. Upon him.

Habakkuk had looked at the coming judgment from God's viewpoint alone. His concern had been for God's glory, and not for men . . . not even for himself. But Habakkuk was a man, and as a man he must face the terror of Chaldea.

This was to be no judgment in the abstract. If he lived, Habakkuk himself would hunger. He would see his loved ones ravaged and in agony. Habakkuk himself would sink in exhaustion beneath the slave's load, or writhe in the fires of his cruel tormentors.

What now, Habakkuk? Still eager to pray for the judgment to come?

Habakkuk has climbed a peak of rock and reasoned with Jehovah. He has seen God's dealings with men who choose sin, and understood His ways. Now Habakkuk is asked to ascend still higher.

No climb up any mountain crag, no gasp for breath or muscle's straining drag, can compare with the agony that grips Habakkuk in this final moment. All his creatureliness cries out against the weight of the divine sentence, seen now to be resting on him. How easy to talk of faith when there is no testing: how hard when every cell screams in the crucible of experience. And Habakkuk knew! Habakkuk had just experienced a vision of judgment. Can this man now throw himself into the arms of the God who decrees his suffering and find rest in Him?

Habakkuk stops struggling, his attention momentarily caught by a small brown figure on the rocks below. A little goat, unawed by the dizzying depths, confidently descends a path invisible to the prophet.

Yes, judgment will come. And Habakkuk himself will often stand on the brink of experience he knows he has no strength to endure. Many will fail, their false faith crumbling under pressures too great for mere humanity.

39

But . . .

Habakkuk rests now.

His eyes look up toward God, and in his heart Habakkuk faces the judgment he has experienced in his vision.

> But I . . .
>   I will exult in Jehovah.
>   I will rejoice in the God of my salvation.
> Jehovah is my sufficiency,
>   and He will continue to place my feet,
>   as He does that mountain goat!
>   so will He cause me to walk in the heights!
>   *Habakkuk 3:18, 19*

Habakkuk has reached the pinnacle of faith.

GOING DEEPER

to personalize

1. Chapter 2 of Habakkuk gives one answer to the problem of evil "triumphing." The text points out that even when the sinner apparently prospers, principles of judgment are already at work in his personality and circumstances.

Look at each of the following sections in the Habakkuk text printed in this chapter, and in a single sentence explain the principle of present judgment already operating. The passages: Hab. 2: 4, 5, 6-8, 9-11, 12-14, 15-17, and 18-20.

2. Habakkuk 3 contains a second and conclusive answer to the problem of the evil prospering. God is

Judge, and will surely judge sin. In this chapter, God reveals Himself as Judge and demonstrates His willingness to intervene by pointing up past interventions in history.

What historical references do these passages seem to you to describe? Locate each in an earlier Old Testament historical portion, and read the descriptions there. What impressions do you develop of God as Judge?

3. Habakkuk's prophecy concerning the Babylonians is not the first to speak of that people. Read Isaiah 39, which describes an incident that took place a hundred or so years before Habakkuk's time.

to probe

1. Locate in Deuteronomy warnings of judgments that were to follow sin by Israel. Discuss in a short paper what seems significant about the passages you chose.

2. In view of the context, what do you believe is the intent of Habakkuk 2:20? Do you think it is an appropriate call to worship for churches today? Why, or why not?

41

TWO KINGDOMS

THROUGH THE EYES OF HABAKKUK we have seen the
tragic state of God's people, poised on the very edge
of judgment. It is over three hundred years since the
glory days of David and Solomon's kingdoms. The
years have been marked by division, by apostasy, by
evil kings and infrequent revivals, by prophets sent
by God to warn His people and call them back to
Him. Yet the ministry of the prophets and even the
leadership of a few godly kings have not been
enough to stay the nation's steady drift away from
God and toward judgment.

Probably the best way to trace this progressive
deterioration of the Hebrew nation is through the
eyes of the prophets God sent to His people. Each
spoke, as did Habakkuk, in a specific historical setting. Each had a definite message to the people of his
own day. Each gives us deep insight into the inner
life of both the individual and of society. Through
the eyes of the prophets we can understand the

influences that broke down the spiritual life and health of the nation—and find help in evaluating influences that affect you and me today. In the prophets' words to people of their own times we hear God's Word to us, calling us to His way of life now.

What was the world of the prophets like? What happened in these 3½ centuries between the death of Solomon (931 B.C.) and the destruction of Jerusalem and exile of the Jews from the Promised Land (586 B.C.)? How did God's people journey toward the edge of judgment?

Israel: the Northern Kingdom (931-722). The times of David and Solomon were days of glory for Israel. Blessed with power and prosperity, the united Jewish nation was a politically dominant nation in the Middle East. But all was not well within Israel. In Solomon's later years, as the weight of his bureaucracy increased and his building projects multiplied, even his great income was not enough. He increased taxes on his people and drafted more and more men as labor levies. Discontent grew.

On Solomon's death, his heir, Rehoboam, went to Shechem to meet with the dissidents. The people came with the intention of making him king. Choosing a spokesman who had been Solomon's enemy (Jeroboam), the people promised to accept Rehoboam as king if he would lighten the tax burden. Foolishly, Rehoboam refused, promising rather to increase the burden. The ten northern tribes then openly rebelled, rejecting the Davidic dynasty's right to reign (2 Chron. 10). In Rehoboam's place, they recognized Jeroboam as king of Israel, and when the prophet Shemaiah turned back a loyalist army, a permanent division between the southern and northern tribes results, forming two nations. They would hereafter be known as Judah (southern) and Israel (northern).

As king of Israel, Jeroboam now faced a difficult political situation. The worship center for the Hebrew people was at Jerusalem, which was also the capital of the Southern Kingdom. Fearing that the people would return to the Davidic dynasty if they made the required annual pilgrimages to the Temple, Jeroboam erected his own "iron curtain" between the two nations and went about setting up a rival religious system (1 Kings 12).

Jeroboam's false system counterfeited the pattern established by God in the Old Testament Law. He established worship centers at Dan and Bethel, but rather than erect temples, he put up idols there— golden calves on whose back the invisible God was imagined to ride. He turned out the Levitical priests, who would not go along with his apostate plans, and ordained whoever would volunteer, setting up his own priestly and sacrificial systems. Finally, copying the great feasts of the Law in which all Hebrews were commanded to participate, Jeroboam instituted his own festivals, set for different times than those God had commanded.

This false religious system had a dual impact on the Northern Kingdom, Israel. First, the godly people slipped over into Judah and settled there so they could worship the Lord as He had commanded

TWO KINGDOMS

	ISRAEL Major Kings	Prophets		JUDAH Major Kings	Prophets
931	Jeroboam I	Ahijah[1] (Unnamed)[2]	931	Rehoboam	Shemaiah[10]
909	Baasha	Jehu[3]	910	Asa	Azariah[11]
886	Omri				
874	Ahab	Elijah[4] (Unnamed)[5] Micaiah[6] Elisha[7] Obadiah	872	Jehoshaphat	Hanani[12] Jehu[13] Jahaziel[14] Eliezer[15] Elijah[16]
841	Jehu		835	Joash	Zechariah[17] Joel
793	Jeroboam II	Jonah[8] Amos Hosea	797 791	Amaziah Uzziah	
			750	Jotham	Isaiah Micah
722		Oded[9]	728	Hezekiah	

Assyrian Captivity

1. 1 Kings 11, 14
2. 1 Kings 13
3. 1 Kings 16
4. 1 Kings 17—2 Kings 2
5. 1 Kings 20
6. 1 Kings 22
7. 1 Kings 19—2 Kings 13
8. also 2 Kings 14
9. 2 Chron. 28
10. 2 Chron. 11, 12
11. 2 Chron. 15
12. 2 Chron. 16
13. 2 Chron. 19
14. 2 Chron. 29
15. 2 Chron. 29
16. 2 Chron. 21
17. 2 Chron. 24

Nahum

640	Josiah	Habakkuk
586		Zephaniah Jeremiah Ezekiel

Babylonian Captivity

them. The immigrants were a significant number: note the size of the army Judah was able to mobilize (400,000, according to 2 Chron. 13:3) contrasted with only 180,000 just eighteen years earlier at the break between the two kingdoms (11:1).

A second impact was on the character of the Northern Kingdom. The first king made a conscious and overtly rebellious decision to break with God and His Law; each succeeding king continued in the pattern Jeroboam set. Israel, with only nineteen kings during its short existence, knew nine different dynasties. Only eight kings died a natural death. Seven were assassinated, one was a suicide, one was killed in battle, one died of injuries suffered in a fall, and the last king, Hoshea, simply disappeared into captivity. The Bible says that they all "did that which was evil in the sight of the Lord."

With this kind of leadership, no wonder the people who remained in the apostate kingdom quickly fell into Baal worship and all sorts of injustice. God continued to send prophets to speak to Israel, but they continued to resent the prophets' ministries and to reject their message.

After a stormy history—during which Israel, however, did know material prosperity under strong rulers such as Omri (who established Israel's capital at Samaria) and Jeroboam II—Israel fell to the Assyrians in 722 B.C. The city of Samaria was totally destroyed and the people of Israel deported. The Northern Kingdom disappeared from history; only the families who had settled in Judah kept the identity of the ten tribes alive.

46

Judah: the Southern Kingdom (931-586 B.C.). The dreary portrait of Israel's experience under the apostate kings is lightened when we look at Judah. Politically, the Southern Kingdom knew its ups and downs as conflicts with Egypt, Israel, and other surrounding states brought alternate victories and defeats. Spiritually, Judah was blessed with several godly kings. But she also knew the rule of apostate kings who followed Solomon's example and permitted pagan worship in the holy land. Queen Athaliah (841-835 B.C.) struggled to introduce the cult of Baal in Judah as her mother Jezebel had in Israel. Yet a succession of God-approved kings (Joash through Jotham) kept the extension of evil tendencies to a minimum.

Still, the great revivals under Kings Asa, Jehoshaphat, and Joash were unable to purify the land. As we saw in our study of Habakkuk, much local autonomy was retained under the kings, and the piety of a ruler did not guarantee the holiness of his people.

Hezekiah, one of the most godly kings, guided Judah during the critical time of Israel's destruction. He instituted drastic reform to correct the idolatry of his father Ahaz and thoroughly cleansed the land. He was certainly influenced by two great prophetic contemporaries, Isaiah and Micah.

Yet Hezekiah's own son, Manasseh, who ruled fifty-five years, was one of Judah's most evil men. He supported pagan worship, recognized the sacrifice of children to the Ammonite god Molech, and killed all who protested. Tradition tells us that Isaiah met

47

his death at Manasseh's hands.

In spite of later revival under Josiah (640-609), king during Habakkuk's days, the religious and moral deterioration was such that the revival made little impact on Judah. The graphic descriptions by Jeremiah and Ezekiel (Ezek. 8—11) of the way of life of God's people helps us see clearly why the announced judgment *must* come.

And come it did. In a series of deportations, the surviving kingdom was wrenched from the land. The Temple and the Holy City were totally destroyed. Under the weight of agonizing chastisement, God's people did come to repentance in a foreign land. There they were purified of idolatry and, finally, a remnant returned from Babylon to the Promised Land to reestablish the Jewish homeland and to await Messiah.

THE PROPHETS

Reading the divine history, we quickly gain the impression that two groups of persons are most significant during the time of the kingdoms. One is the rulers, whose deeds and misdeeds are chronicled. The other is the prophets, whose voices were raised at critical times in each nation's experience.

Who were these prophets, and what was their ministry?

While the original sense of the word is unclear, its use in Scriptures gives us a clear definition. A prophet is a spokesman for God. An incident in Exodus helps us see this role. Moses had been called by God to deliver Israel, yet he feared that because he did not speak fluently he would not be able to move Pharaoh. God promised to give him Aaron, his brother, as "a mouth." "He shall speak for you to the people; and he shall be a mouth for you, and you shall be to him as God" (Exod. 4:16, RSV). This relationship is further described by God in Exodus 7:1: "See, I made you as God to Pharaoh, and Aaron your brother shall be your prophet."

As Moses was God's spokesman, Aaron was to be his. In a similar relationship, prophets in the time of the two kingdoms served as "God's mouth."

The prophetic ministry was not one in which the spokesman's personality was blotted out in some ecstatic mystical experience. Each prophet retained his own individuality, his own personality and peculiarities. Each spoke in his own historical and cultural context. Yet each was God's spokesman; each communicated God's own message.

Scripture gives us insights into how the prophets received their messages. At times they seem to have heard an external voice (1 Sam. 3:3-9). Often the voice was internal (Hab. 2:1; Isa. 7:3, 4). Then again, the prophet was enabled to see spiritual realities invisible to others (Num. 22:31; 2 Kings 6:15-17). At other times the prophets saw visions (Ezek. 37, 40—48). The message was received in many ways, but the true spokesman recognized its source and confidently announced that what he had to say was "the word of the Lord."

Often, during the days of the two kingdoms, the ministry of the prophets was directed to the rulers.

49

This was true of earlier days as well. Nathan the prophet rebuked David (2 Sam. 12), as did Gad (ch. 24). It was Samuel, the prophet-judge, who ministered to Saul and anointed David king. Because the kings chose to move away from God, meetings between prophet and ruler often became a confrontation. On the day that Jeroboam instituted his false religion, he was confronted by "a man of God from Judah" (1 Kings 13:1). This prophet announced judgment on the altar Jeroboam was consecrating, foretelling the birth of Joash, a king of Judah, who would one day burn the bones of the false priests upon it. He gave a sign to prove that he was speaking by God's command: the altar would crack, and the ashes spill out. Angered, Jeroboam commanded that the young prophet be seized. But the hand he stretched out was gripped by paralysis: he could not lower it! And at that moment, the altar split.

Cowed, Jeroboam begged the prophet to ask God to release his paralysis, and the hand was restored. God's spokesman then made his announcements with full authority.

Such miracles or soon-fulfilled prophecy often authenticated the prophets. The influence they wielded is shown by the fact that Rehoboam turned back an army about to attack the rebellious Israel at the word of Shemaiah (2 Chron. 11), and even Jeroboam, when his son became ill, sent his wife to the prophet Abijah to inquire of the Lord (1 Kings 14).

The ministry of the prophet was often resented by rebellious kings, and their message was often rejected. But kings—godly and ungodly—and the common people as well, recognized these men as God's spokesman and viewed them with awe and often fear.

How is it then that the prophets were unable to halt the slide of the kingdoms into sin? Why was their ministry largely ineffective?

As today, the problem lay not with the Word but with the hearer. These spokesmen for God did deliver His message. But the people did not respond with faith. They recognized the message and the messenger as from God, but this awareness did not lead them to commitment. Unwilling to submit to God's way, the people stubbornly held to their own paths. It is not, as Jesus reminds us, the one who hears the Word of God but the one who *hears and does* who is blessed (Matt. 7:24).

The men and women of the two kingdoms, who took pride in their religious activities, their prophets, their Temple and holy men, were all too like men and women of today who confuse church-going with discipleship, "Bible-believing" with obedience. In the prophetic call to God's people to respond to Him and wholeheartedly obey, we hear His invitation to us today—an invitation designed not to burden us, but to lead us safely away from the edge of that personal judgment to which our willful choices would most certainly lead.

GOING DEEPER

This week explore the Bible's description of the

division of the Hebrew nation into the Northern and Southern Kingdoms. Meet some of the prophets whose ministry at that crucial time introduces us so well to the office of these spokesmen for the Lord.

to personalize

1. From 1 Kings 11:26—14:20, develop a personality profile of Jeroboam, first ruler of the Northern Kingdom. Be careful and thorough.

2. From the same passage, particularly 12:26—13:6, list the actions Jeroboam took to establish his kingdom, which in effect led Israel away from God.

3. Two prophets play significant roles in the story of the establishment of the Northern Kingdom. From the description of Abijah and his ministry, and of the "man of God who came from Judah," list everything you observe that helps you understand the prophets' role. (Include at least twenty items on your list.)

to probe

1. Look up at least five prophets who ministered *before* 931 B.C. Study the passages telling about them. What additional information do you gain about the prophets?

2. Study the life of Samuel and his ministry as a prophet. What do you learn about the prophet from this man?

3. Read two books that describe or explain the role of the prophet in the Old Testament.

CONFRONTED!

ISRAEL WAS BORN IN REBELLION and nursed in apostasy. Yet there was worse to come.

A series of assassinations in 886 B.C. led to the crowning of Omri, a ranking army officer. Capable and aggressive, Omri quickly stablized the nation. He built and fortified Samaria as capital and so impressed the Assyrians that a hundred years later Israel was known by them as the "land of Omri."

The Bible tells us little about Omri's reign (1 Kings 16: 23-27), but archeology has added several important bits of information. An inscribed pillar, the Moabite Stone, found in 1898, reports that Omri conquered Moab and forced it to pay tribute to Israel. The marriage of his son Ahab to the Phoenician princess Jezebel indicates close relationships with Phoenicia, a valuable trading ally for Israel. It is likely that much of the wealth of Samaria revealed by archeological expeditions has root in the diplomacy and statecraft of Omri.

Yet in Scripture, the focus clearly is not on the political and economic affairs of God's people; the focus instead is placed on the religious and moral dimensions of life. And here Omri's key significance seems to have been that he fathered Ahab, who was without question the most evil ruler yet.

Ahab's reign. As a political and military leader, Ahab receives good marks. He was effective in defeating Israel's Syrian enemies, joined in a coalition army which halted the invasion of a great Assyrian force under Shalmaneser III, and maintained the borders of his land. Assyrian records tell us that Ahab was able to contribute 2,000 chariots (the tanks of ancient warfare) to the coalition army as well as some 10,000 foot soldiers.

Economically, Israel also prospered. The Phoenician alliance meant that sea trade routes were open to landlocked Israel, and the great "ivory house" Ahab built for himself (1 Kings 22:39) testifies to the land's prosperity.

Yet that same Phoenician alliance opened the door to the introduction of Baal worship in Israel. Ahab's marriage to Jezebel, a devotee of Baal, forced a direct confrontation. Jezebel was not satisfied with coexistence: she insisted that Baal worship replace any worship of Jehovah. She not only slaughtered the Hebrew prophets of Jehovah (1 Kings 18:4); she also imported hundreds of prophets of Baal to establish worship centers for this pagan deity.

Baal-Melquart, commonly called simply Baal in this part of Scripture, was the expression of Baal worshiped in Tyre, Jezebel's home city. The term *baal* means simply "owner" or "lord". In Canaan, the Baals were nature gods, regarded as owners of particular localities, and believed to control fertility. Thus good crops as well as the human birth rate demanded that a people be on good terms with the local "owner" deity.

As Canaanite religion developed, focusing on the cycles of the year, extreme cult activities were required to ensure the giving of the needed rains. These included prostitution of both sexes as a prominent feature (see Jer. 7:9, Amos 2:7, and Judg. 2:17) and even child sacrifice (Jer. 19:5). These orgiastic religious practices are well documented in hymns and poems from the period, which show a deadening moral depravity associated with religious worship.

Jezebel and Ahab went about imposing this entire system on Israel, aggressively seeking to blot out the worship of Jehovah.

Standing against such complete apostasy and thwarting the attempt of those in power was the best known of Old Testament prophets, Elijah. With others, he continually confronted the king and his pagan consort and called Israel to commitment to God.

THE PROPHETS
Deuteronomy 18:9-22

When, under Moses' leadership, God's people were about to enter the land of Palestine, God gave implicit instructions about supernatural guidance. The Canaanite peoples practiced witchcraft, consulted spiritualists, and used other means of divining the future. All such sources were forbidden to God's people, who had His Word to live by. And in this key passage of Scripture they were promised that when God wanted to communicate to them, He would raise up a prophet (vs. 15). Such spokesmen for God would report His Word to the people; the people were to listen and obey.

This promise of prophetic guidance included several tests by which a true prophet of God was to be recognized.

Recognizing prophets. Prophets whom God actually did send were marked off in several special ways.

1. The prophet was to be "from among you, from your countrymen" (Deut. 18:15). No foreigner could speak to God's people in God's name; the Phoenician prophets of Baal were automatically ruled out.

2. The prophet would speak "in the name of the Lord" (18:20-22). Any prophet who claimed to have a supernatural message to communicate but delivered it as a message from another god was to be killed.

3. The prophet would predict events which invariably came true. Any self-proclaimed prophet whose message told of a future event that did not come true could be safely ignored.

Bible history shows us that this is a very significant test. Often when prophets spoke about the far-distant time of Messiah, they included a short-term prophecy as well. When the short-term prophecy was fulfilled, the hearers had authentication of the long-range message as well.

Thus, the spokesmen God sent to his people would be Hebrews, they would claim their message was from the Lord, and their claim would be authenticated by 100 percent fulfillment of predictions.

One additional test is given in Deuteronomy 13—a test which warns against acceptance of the miraculous as sufficient evidence of God's hand. The Bible says, "If a prophet arises among you, or a dreamer of dreams, and gives you a sign or wonder and the sign or wonder he speaks about comes to pass, and he then says to you, 'Let us go after other gods . . .' do not listen to the words of that prophet" (13:1-3, Modern Language Bible).

The point is clear: the prophet's message must be in harmony with the written Word (see 13:3-5). If from God, the prophet's message will be in full harmony with previous revelation.

This is an important point for us to remember today, even as it was for Israel and Judah. There *are* supernatural powers in conflict with God. A miraculous event or a fulfilled prediction is not in itself a sure evidence that God is behind the sign. The content of the message must always be measured against the teaching of God's Word; where they stand in conflict, the written Word is given unquestioned precedence.

False prophets. In actual fact, Israel did know counterfeit prophets, even as today we know counterfeit religious leaders. Some were men who prophesied in the name of an idol (see Jer. 2:8, 23:13, and 1 Kings 18). Others pretended to be prophets to win the favor of rulers like Ahab, as in 1 Kings 22, when the false prophets were quick to give him the message they knew he wanted to hear. Others very possibly spoke in God's name but were sharing messages from a different source.

In times when prophetic activity was high—as in the days of Ahab and Jezebel—it might have been easy for confusion to grow over who the true and false prophets were. Yet, marked off by the tests we have seen above and authenticated as well by the work of God within the hearer, God's spokesmen *were* recognized. The message they shared was known to come from God. But all too often the message, like God Himself, was ignored.

ELIJAH

The biblical report of Ahab's reign is intertwined with a portrait of the prophets who constantly confronted him. Later, we will trace the interplay between ruler and prophets in the Bible text itself; here we will simply note highlights that may make the Bible's report more clear.

1 Kings 17:1–18:15. Elijah's background is not explained, except that he was a settler of Gilead. We meet him when he was sent to Ahab to announce that for three years no rain or dew would touch Israel until Elijah himself said so.

This particular judgment is significant. The Baal worship Ahab and Jezebel were promoting was a fertility faith: the worship of Baal was justified as guaranteeing rains and crops. Now Jehovah challenged Baal at the very point at which his strength was supposed to lie.

1 Kings 18:16-46. The drought did not convince Israel of Baal's impotence. So Elijah was commanded to engineer a direct confrontation. Eight hundred fifty prophets of Baal and Asherah met him on Mount Carmel. After a whole day of futile prayer by the pagan prophets, God answered Elijah's simple prayer and in a blazing holocaust burned not only the offering laid out on a water-soaked altar but also the very stones of the altar itself.

Convinced, the watching crowds killed the pagan prophets who had been polluting God's people and land.

Following this choice by Israel, Elijah announced the return of the rains.

1 Kings 19. Elijah's flight after victory shows us again the humanness of the prophets. Like us, their great triumphs were often followed by depression.

God ministered to Elijah as He does to us and led him out again to serve.

Elijah's place in Scripture. C. E. DeVries in the *Zondervan Pictorial Encyclopedia* summarizes the many references to Elijah in later Scriptures.

Malachi 4:5 foretold that Elijah would appear again before the day of the Lord; this prediction has both New Testament and future fulfillment (cf. Rev. 11:6). The annunciatory angel declared to Zechariah that his son, John the Baptist, would go before the Lord in "the spirit and power of Elijah" (Luke 1:17). Though John denied that he was Elijah (John 1:21, 15), Jesus spoke of John as "Elijah who is to come" (Matt. 11:14; 17:10-13).

Elijah appeared as a participant in the scene of the Transfiguration, when he and Moses discussed with the Lord the "departure" which Jesus was to accomplish at Jerusalem (Matt. 17:4; Mark 9:5; Luke 9:33).

Paul, arguing for the principle of a remnant of Israel, referred to the 7,000 faithful worshippers in the time of Elijah (Rom. 11:2-4). The two witnesses of Rev. 11 are not mentioned by name, but the powers ascribed to them are those of Moses and Elijah (vs. 6).

Vol. 2, p. 287

As we read the Old Testament account, it is helpful to realize that we are reading of a man whom the rest of Scripture marks out as particularly significant.

1 Kings 20. There were other prophets in Israel during these days. This account shows a positive ministry of a unnamed prophet and the response of a desperate Ahab. Only after the enemy is defeated does Ahab, released from the grip of fear, revert to type and reject God's commands.

1 Kings 21. The incident of Naboth's vineyard gives further insight into Ahab's character and the judgment of God that Elijah pronounces on the wicked family.

1 Kings 22. Three years after God's sentence on Ahab is pronounced, the evil king of Israel meets the foretold doom. The story of Micaiah's prophetic role is particularly interesting. First we see his boldness in a sarcastic response to the king, which was recognized as such by Ahab (vss. 15, 16). Another feature is Micaiah's revelation from the spirit world and the clear indication that spirits may *deceive*. Even given the supernatural origin of much of the occult activity of our day, there is no guarantee that such spirits have man's best interests at heart. In fact, only God Himself can be trusted to act in love and justice in our lives.

THE END OF THE DYNASTY
2 Kings 1:1–10:17

Ahab's death did not put an end to Jezebel's efforts on behalf of Baal. The ruling family was still strong . . . but its days were limited.

After Elijah had been transported to heaven without dying (2 Kings 2:11-13), his successor, Elisha, took up the battle. Leading the "sons of the prophets," a group many commentators believe was made up of men studying for spiritual leadership (as in a modern seminary), Elisha throughout his life played a significant part in the political, military, and spiritual life of the land. God continued to aid his people in their ceaseless warfare with Syria, and finally, in accordance with Elijah's early prophecy, the entire family of Ahab was exterminated by Jehu, who also totally wiped out the worship of Baal.

61

GOING DEEPER

to personalize

1. Read *rapidly* 1 Kings 16 through 2 Kings 11 to get a picture of the interplay between the ruling family of Ahab and God's prophets. Afterward, jot down on a piece of paper your dominant impressions.

2. Deuteronomy 13:1-5 and 18:9-22 explain something of the prophet's ministry and distinguishing characteristics. List the four evidences of a true prophet found in these texts; from 1 Kings 16-22, show how Elijah met each.

3. How do you believe contemporary interest in the occult compares with similar interest in Old Testament times? From the Deuteronomy passage, how would you say a believer should react to such things as spiritists and Ouija boards, tarot cards, and astrology, etc.? Why?

4. If you were teaching a Bible study on the life of Elijah, what five important lessons for us today would you stress?

5. Make a chart comparing and contrasting all the prophets we meet in 1 Kings 16 through 2 Kings 11. Study each carefully to decide what factors should be compared and contrasted before developing your chart.

to probe

Most of our attention in this study is focused on Elijah and Ahab. For your *probe* studies, focus on Elisha and the last days of Ahab's family (2 Kings 1—11).

1. From the biblical text, outline the military events in Israel. What was life in the land like?

2. List the fourteen miracles attributed to Elisha: choose two of them to study in depth. What was the purpose of each miracle you chose? What did it tell Israel about God?

3. Select three incidents from which you believe good sermons or devotional studies might be constructed. For each passage, (a) express in a single sentence what you would teach from it; (b) express in a single sentence what response you would seek from your hearers. Then, (c) for *one* of the three passages develop a one-page outline of the message or devotional.

4. Select one person from the overall section (Ahab, Jezebel, Elijah, or Elisha) and do a five- to- seven-page biographical study. Be sure to include lessons we can learn from the person's life.

RUNAWAY

SOME THIRTY YEARS BEFORE the Assyrians destroyed the Northern Kingdom, the prophet Jonah
was sent from Israel to save the enemy capital.

Jonah lived and ministered during the golden age
of the Northern Kingdom. Under Jeroboam II, a
weakened Israel saw a dramatic resurgence of
power, and Jonah had a dramatic role in this recovery. Second Kings 14 tells us that while Jeroboam
"did not depart from all the sins of Jeroboam the son
of Nebat" (the first Jeroboam), nevertheless, "he
restored the border of Israel from the entrance of
Hamath as far as the Sea of the Arabah, *according to
the word of the Lord, the God of Israel, which he spoke by his
servant Jonah* the son of Amittai, the prophet, who
was from Gath-hepher" (vss. 24, 25, RSV).

Jonah apparently had a patriotic and popular
ministry. He must have enjoyed the favor of both
Jeroboam II and his people.

No wonder the divine command to go to Nineveh, the capital of the empire that for decades had terrorized the peoples of Palestine, came as a jolting shock. The Bible indicates that Jonah reacted immediately to the divine commission: "Jonah rose up to flee unto Tarshish from the presence of the Lord" (Jon. 1:3).

The prophet had acted as God's spokesman when the message was a good one for his people. But he was unwilling to carry a message to an enemy who might do them harm!

THE STORY

We are all familiar with Jonah's experience. Going to the seaport at Joppa, he took a ship for Tarshish, in Spain, as far away from Nineveh as he could travel. But God stayed with this runaway. A storm struck, which terrified even the ship's experienced crew. Recalling that Jonah had told them he was fleeing from God (1:10), the mariners took Jonah's advice and reluctantly threw him over the side. The storm calmed immediately, and Jonah sank beneath the waves.

Slipping down, his body entangled by the fronds of giant, fifty-foot-long seaweeds, Jonah was sure that death was God's judgment on his disobedience. Then, suddenly, he found himself swallowed by a giant fish. He lost consciousness—later waking to realize he still lived and that the fish had been prepared by God to save his life. Later, Jonah would pen a psalm about his experiences:

65

While I was fainting away,
I remembered the Lord;
And my prayer came to Thee
Into Thy holy temple.

Jonah 2:7

The giant fish bore the repentant prophet back the way he'd come and vomited him up on dry land. And the Bible tells us, "Now the word of the Lord came to Jonah the second time, saying, 'Arise, go to Nineveh the great city and proclaim to it the proclamation which I am going to tell you'" (3: 1, 2).

Obediently, Jonah now trudged toward the enemy capital to fulfill God's command.

The Nineveh of Jonah's day was a great city; counting its suburbs, it took three days to walk through it. That first day, Jonah began to shout out the message God gave him: "Yet forty days, and Nineveh will be overthrown!" (3: 4, RSV)

The pagan people of Nineveh did not laugh at this strange little Jewish fanatic. Instead, they "believed God, and proclaimed a fast, and put on sackcloth, from the greatest of them even to the least of them" (3: 5). The message of coming judgment had immediate effect and brought a wholehearted repentance.

Scholars who have studied Assyrian history have suggested possible reasons for this response. Under Adad-Nirari III (c. 810—783 B.C.) the Assyrians had begun a trend toward monotheism. And just before the probable time of Jonah's arrival, a great plague had marked the reign of Assurdan III (c. 771—754

B.C.). Whatever the contributing factors, the Assyrians did respond to God's message. King, nobles, and slaves fasted, mourned, and prayed, humbling themselves before God.

And when God saw that they did turn away from their wicked way, "God relented concerning the calamity which He had declared He would bring upon them" (3:10).

After delivering his message of impending doom, Jonah slipped out of the city. Finding hilly ground to the east, he settled down to wait and see what God would do. Nothing happened. Jonah reacted with anger and bitterness. His complaint opens up the motive for his earlier flight to Tarshish. "Please Lord, was this not what I said while I was still in my own country? Therefore, in order to forestall this, I fled to Tarshish, for I knew that Thou art a gracious and compassionate God, slow to anger and abundant in lovingkindness, and One who relents concerning calamity" (4:2).

Jonah, who had prophesied before on behalf of "my own country," now asked God to take his life rather than let him live to remember that he might have been used to deliver his country's enemy.

So he settled down, despite the intense heat, to wait out the forty days, still hoping to see Nineveh destroyed. God then caused a plant to grow which was large and succulent enough to shelter the prophet, and Jonah was "extremely happy" (v. 6). But the next day God caused a worm to attack the plant, and it withered away. That day was agonizing, with a scorching wind and a sun that beat unmercifully down on Jonah's head. Exhausted by the sun and heat, the suffering Jonah begged God to let him die, insisting that he had every right to be angry about the plant as well as about his mission to the city.

The book concludes with God's words of instruction to Jonah—words the prophet faithfully recorded although they constitute a sharp rebuke. Jonah cared about the plant, a thing of transitory existence at best. And God asks, "Should I not have compassion on Nineveh, the great city in which there are more than 120,000 persons who do not know the difference between their right hand and left hand (e.g., tiny infants), as well as many animals?" (4:11, NASB).

God's compassion extends to all. Persons are important to Him.

MESSAGES

The Book of Jonah is far more complex than it seems at first glance. The basically simple story communicates messages to us on many different levels.

The relationship between God and unbelieving nations. On one level, Jonah portrays God's way of dealing with Gentile nations while working with Israel through His Covenant and Law. It is clear from the Book of Jonah that God has *not* simply "set aside" the nations as unimportant or their peoples as without value.

1. God clearly cared about the Gentiles during this

period when the Jews were His Chosen People. God's heart was moved with compassion for Nineveh and its inhabitants.

2. God also maintained a moral relationship with those who were not His own. The Ninevites were responsible for their actions, and God took the responsibility to judge them when they sinned. It is also clear from the response of the Ninevites that they were aware of what constituted wickedness. While God did not hold them responsible for Israel's Law, it is clear that they were being judged on the basis of what light they did possess (see Romans 2:12-16).

3. It is also clear that God gave them sufficient information about Himself and His intentions for them to respond. We must never think that even pagan peoples today have *no* light.

4. Finally, we see striking evidence that God was—and is—responsive to the unbeliever as well as the believer. He heard the prayer of these men even though they were without personal relationship with Him. God's goodness extends far beyond our understanding.

We must be careful not to push these observations too far, yet it is important to realize that while God was dealing with the Hebrew people throughout the course of Old Testament history, and while they *are* His Chosen People, God still maintained a supervisory relationship with all. He still cared for all.

The relationship between God and Jonah as an individual. Two striking relationships are illustrated. The first has to do with God's commitment to His

69

own. Jonah ran away from God, willfully and consciously disobeying the divine command. God's response was to *stay with* His runaway. He disciplined Jonah, but only to bring the straying prophet back into renewed fellowship with Him. And after Jonah had returned to God, God gave Jonah a second chance.

The idea of a second chance is something we often lose sight of. We tend to feel that sin and disobedience disqualify us from further service. Jonah shows us how full and free God's forgiveness really is. He forgives and *restores*. In fellowship with God again, we can be both useful and fulfilled.

A second important message communicated to us in the relationship between God and Jonah has to do with God's attitude toward the believer. Jonah was a prophet with a message, but Jonah was not just a tool. After the prophet's work was done, God continued to deal with Jonah as an individual.

And God's concern was focused not on Jonah's behavior but on his values and attitudes—his inner character.

The Book of Jonah shows Jonah as a man without compassion for his enemies. He did care about "us." But he wished only evil on "them." While Jonah obeyed God when given his second chance, his heart was not in tune with the Lord. Yet it is our heart that God cares about; He seeks not mere obedience, but that we *become like Him*.

One day Jesus would teach in the Sermon on the Mount, "Love your enemies" (Matt. 5:43), and He would point out that in loving our enemies the disci-

RUNAWAY!

CHORUS (v.1,2,3)
Oh, run-a-way, run-a-way, run-a-way___, Jon-ah runs all
Yes, run-a-way, run-a-way, run-a-way, Some-times we run all

CHORUS (v.4)
Oh, run-a-way, run-a-way, run-a-way___, run right back to
Yes, run-a-way, run-a-way, run-a-way, We run right back to

day, But God is run-ning with him and with Jon-ah God will stay.
day, But God is run-ning with us and ___ with us God will stay.
God. For God still loves a run-a-way ___ says, "Come to Me to-day."
God. For God still loves a run-a-way ___ we come to God to-day.

1. God's road goes to Nin-e-veh. But Jon-ah shouts out, (pause) "No!"
2. ___ Jon-ah's on the o-cean wide. The storm fills all with fear.
3. ___ Jon-ah's deep in-side the fish And Jon-ah cries out, "Lord!"
4. ___ Jon-ah goes to Nin-e-veh. He warns the peo-ple there.

"I'll trav-el on my own road, God.___ That's the way I'll go."
When Jon-ah's tossed over the side...God's fish is wait-ing near.
"I see now that your road is best...___ That's the road I wish."
They all ___ quick-ly turn to God, ___ God the cit-y spares.

ple is like the heavenly Father, who gives His rain to just and unjust alike.

That was no new revelation.

The Book of Jonah reverberates with the same message: God has compassion on all people, even those who make themselves His enemies and the enemies of His people. And the believer is to be like God in His love for and valuing of all men.

The relationship between God and Israel. The nation Israel had known the ministry of many significant prophets, all warning them to return to God. And, like Jonah, Israel had resolutely run the other way.

Following Jonah, or perhaps contemporary with him, Amos shouted out his pronouncements of judgment on the wickedness of God's people. In the experience of Jonah, Israel was given two significant object lessons that reveal God's willingness to forgive.

First, Jonah himself demonstrated the willingness of God to restore fellowship and to work with the repentant individual, shaping his character toward godliness. If Israel would follow Jonah's course and return to God, the nation could expect its compassionate God to bless and restore her as well. Second, the example of the Ninevites demonstrated the kind of response that is appropriate to a message of judgment. There must be a turning from the wicked way and a wholehearted humbling before the Lord in repentance. With this repentance comes relief from the sentence of judgment. The foretold evil does not come to pass.

In the Book of Jonah, both individual and national object lessons were given to the men and women of Israel, and thus a promise of restoration was extended. God's heart of compassion had been revealed. Israel—and you and I—*never need fear to return to Him.*

The more we explore the book, the more we see. Once again, and in a simple way, God has communicated many vital principles and messages to us in His Word.

A SPECIAL NOTE

One of the important contributions of Jonah has to do with the interpretation of prophecies concerning judgment. God did *not* do what He announced through His spokesman to Nineveh. Does this mean that Jonah was a false prophet, because what he announced did not come to pass? Does it mean that God changed His mind about the destruction of the city?

It seems clear from the Book of Jonah that prophecies concerning judgment *as they relate to a given generation* are intrinsically conditional; they depend on the response or lack of response to the message.

Perhaps it is best to think of prophecies of judgment in terms of "intercept points." As shown in the figure below, judgment comes when a person or nation passes through the warning zone and reaches a point at which judgment *must be imposed.* If those approaching judgment turn back, they do not experience the judgment they surely would have, had

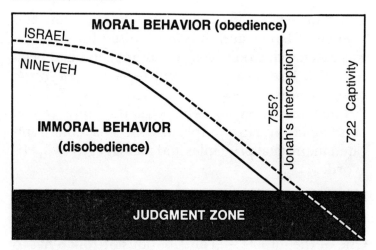

they continued. God did not change his mind; the people changed their direction.

In this sense prophecy, like all revelation, strips away the illusions that cloud men's minds and demonstrates reality. We live in a moral universe, governed by a moral Being. The moral principles on which this universe operates are very similar to the physical laws which govern matter—the principles that give our universe stability. Drop a rock, and according to the physical law of gravity, it will fall—not rise. If we sin or seek by fraud to gain security, according to the inner laws that govern the human personality, only anxiety will come. If we choose, as have many nations in our world's history, a course of international lawlessness and brutality, we will inexorably come to the edge of judgment.

Prophetic warnings announce what will happen when that edge is reached. Sometimes they announce that it is too late; the edge has been passed

74

and impending judgment is sweeping down (Habakkuk). Sometimes the Word comes before we reach the brink, and warns us away. If we respond then, we avoid the fall. God has not changed His mind; we have changed our ways.

Jonah, a short and simple book, was rich in meaning for Jonah's countrymen. It is full of significance for us as well.

GOING DEEPER

to personalize

1. The chart form on page 76 is a tool to enrich your personal study of Jonah. Finish filling it in as you study the book (or reproduce the form on a larger sheet of paper). Use the open spaces to record your observations. Note carefully the contrasts and comparisons between sections of the book. Turn in your chart next class period.

2. Music is a significant way to communicate the message of Bible incidents. "Runaway Song" (71) was written by the author for a Sunday school curriculum. Sing it through a few times, and jot down at least six different values and six different uses for such a teaching song.

3. Study Jonah 2 carefully, noting the sequence of Jonah's feelings as expressed or implied. List *in order* one-word expressions of each feeling you can identify.

Then think about your own experience. Have you ever worked through a similar sequence? Or have you come to a particular point and not moved

THE BOOK OF JONAH

Chapter titles ▸					Nineveh's Repentance			Jonah's complaint	
Notes ▸									
Paragraph titles ▸	1:1-3	4-10	11-16	17	2:1-9	10	3:1-4	5-9	10	4:1-5	6-11
God, characterized by His actions ▸					Deliverer				
Jonah, characterized by his actions ▸		Disobedient							
Main message ▸									

beyond?

What do you think God intends us to learn from this section of His Word?

4. From your chart and chapter, list the personal applications you can make from the Book of Jonah. Which do you feel is most important to you, and why?

to probe

Research one of these two questions:

Was Jonah's being swallowed by the fish a historical event?

Is Jonah a type of Christ?

FOR THREE TRANSGRESSIONS

THE FITFUL WARFARE WITH SYRIA, which had flared up time and time again since the days of Elijah and Elisha, was over. The hundred-year feud was settled and the military threat ended when Damascus came under the sovereignty of Jeroboam II. Israel's territory pushed out almost to the borders of the kingdom of David's day.

An economic explosion took place, much like the stunning revival of West Germany and Japan after World War II. Israel now controlled ancient trade routes, and expansion gave rise to a new social class of wealthy merchants. Wealth created a demand for the many luxuries now available from all over the known world.

Pressured by the influx of wealth, jolting social changes took place. The population began to shift from farms to cities and towns. Class distinctions crystallized, with the rich bent on piling up profits at the expense of their poorer brothers. Exorbitant prices were charged; poor farmers were dispossessed so that the rich might build up great estates. A heartless unconcern for the sufferings of the oppressed marked the well-to-do.

Harley[1] portrays social conditions as sketched by Amos:

> The luxury of the wealthy class in Israel is clearly indicated by the prophet as he speaks of their "couches" and "silken cushions" (3:12), of their "winter-house" and "summer-house," and the "houses of ivory" (ivory inlay and ornamentation), and of "the houses of hewn-stone" (3:15; 5:11). The voluptuous women were spoken of as "kine of Bashan," who insisted that their husbands provide ample wine and other luxuries for their feasts, even if the poor had to be crushed in order to provide these (4:1-3). Their feasts were characterized by revelry, songs, music, choice meats, and the best of wines to satiate their lusts, and by cushions and silken tapestries upon which to recline (6:1-7). These luxuries were enjoyed by the wealthy, whose eyes were closed to the afflictions and needs of the poor (6:6).

The moral condition of the nation is clearly revealed by the prophet's shock at the cruel treatment of the poor by the rich, at the covetousness, injustice, and immorality of the people in power, and at the general contempt for things holy (2:6-8). Trampling on the poor, taking exactions of wheat (5:11), afflicting the just, taking a bribe, and turning aside

1. Homer Harley, *A Commentary on the Minor Prophets* (Grand Rapids: Baker, 1972).

the needy (5:23) stirred the indignation of the prophet and give us an insight into the morals of the day. They were ready to "swallow up the needy" and cause "the poor of the land to fail"—that is, to die (8:4).

In political circles there was tumult and oppression, violence and robbery (3:9-10). People hated any judge who would reprove or speak uprightly (5:10).

Then suddenly, against this background of prosperity and oppression, a man who knew poverty appeared from Judah. For a few short months, he denounced the sins of Israel and promised judgment.

Amos was a native of Tekoa, a town about twelve miles south of Jerusalem. A farmer and herder, he had spent his life caring for sheep and harvesting the sycamore fig, the "food of the poor." He was used to hard work and accustomed to a frugal life. He stood in sharp contrast to the "beautiful people" of Israel.

Shocked by the moral, social, and religious situation in the Northern Kingdom, Amos stood at Bethel (the center of worship established over a century before by Jeroboam I) and denounced the life-style of Israel. In a series of scathing sermons, he confronted the wealthy and ruling classes, exposed their sins, and pronounced in flaming anger the punishment that God was to impose.

Amos's anger was but a pale reflection of God's own wrath. Yet the prosperous of Israel were unmoved. To these proud and selfish men, unconcerned about the misery of those they oppressed, Amos must have seemed some wild fanatic. He was out of touch with modern times—perhaps simply jealous that he was himself poor and not one of the favored few. Later, Jesus would comment to his disciples, "How hard it is for the rich to enter the kingdom of God!" (Luke 18:24, NIV). Prosperity promotes values in deep conflict with what God Himself says is important. How hard it is to have wealth and status, and retain perspective!

THE BOOK OF AMOS

Our Old Testament Book of Amos is a carefully organized compilation of the messages which Amos, God's spokesman to the rich society, delivered in the Northern Kingdom. An outline of the book helps us see its development, and also guides us in reading it today.

AMOS

I. Judgment announced
   A. On the surrounding nations   1:3—2:3
   B. On Israel and Judah   2:4-16
II. Sermons of indictment
   A. First sermon   3:1-15
   B. Second sermon   4:1-13
   C. Third sermon   5:1—6:14
III. Declarations of judgment
   A. The locust plague: judgment averted 7:1-3
   B. The fire: judgment delayed   7:4-6
   C. The plumb line: judgment determined 7:7-9
   D. Amaziah's opposition   7:10-17
   E. The summer fruit: judgment imminent 8:1-14
   F. The broken lintel: judgment executed 9:1-10
IV. Restoration promised   9:11-15

As you follow the outline, the pattern of Amos's preaching becomes sharp and clear.

Outlining. Outlining is one of the basic methods of Bible study. It helps us not only trace a writer's thoughts but also highlights what is important.

For instance, in the first chapter of Amos each of Amos's pronouncements follows a particular pattern:

a. declaration of judgment
b. cause of judgment
c. description of judgment

In speaking against Damascus, Gaza, and on then to Judah and Israel, this pattern is consistently followed.

What seems to be the underlying cause of the judgment pronounced on God's own people?

In Judah, the cause is simple: "because they have rejected the law of the Lord and have not kept his statutes" (2:4b, RSV).

For Israel, the cause is expressed in much greater detail, and the focus is placed squarely on similar violations expressed as societal injustice, the breakdown of morality, and the repudiation of God and His Word. How graphic the words of Amos are:

> "For three transgressions of Israel and for four
> I will not revoke its punishment,
> Because they sell the righteous for money
> And the needy for a pair of sandals.
> These who pant after the very dust of the earth
>   on the head of the helpless
> Also turn aside the way of the humble;

And a man and his father resort to the same girl
In order to profane My holy name.
And on garments taken as pledges they stretch
out beside every altar,
And in the house of their God they drink the
wine of those who have been fined."

Amos 2:6-8

What specifically do these charges reveal?

"They sell the righteous." The rights of the poor,
carefully protected in the Old Testament Law, were
regularly violated. This institutionalized injustice
had turned away the "humble" from following
God's way of love and obedience. It is hard for the
oppressed to love the oppressor!

"A man and his father . . ." This may be a reference
to use of the same temple prostitute. If so, it was a
flagrant violation both of God's command to worship only Him, and a revelation of the gross immorality with pagan worship involved.

"Garments taken as pledges . . ." Here Amos returns
to his central theme of injustice. The Law demanded
that if a poor man's cloak were taken as a pledge
against a loan or debt, it was to be returned to him
before night, since the cloak was also his blanket
(Deut. 24:12, 13). But in Israel, such cloaks were
piled around the altars as resting places for wealthy
worshipers!

"The wine of those who have been fined . . ." Wine that
had been extorted as taxes or fines from the poor
was used in the very centers (wrongly) set aside to
worship God! Thus, even God was made to seem a

party to oppression.

This explanation of the cause of judgment on Israel sets the stage for our reading of the book, and it immediately draws our attention to God's anger and to the causes of His wrath.

AMOS TODAY

The Book of Amos, expressing as it does God's outrage against a society that had become insensitive to justice—a society that materialistically exalted profit over people—has been identified as one of the most significant prophetic books for us today. Certainly, we, too, experience unequalled prosperity. Surely, there are great class distinctions in our society. And surely, too, there is oppression— oppression that has not been touched by institutionalizing a financial dole to the poor.

Perhaps most important, Amos helps us review our own values. He asks the question: does our life-style reflect the heart of God? Or do we share the selfish heart of the indifferent of Amos's day?

Oppression. Reading through Amos, we realize that God's anger constantly flashes out against those who oppress others. The poor of the land seem very precious to Him. The indifferent attitude of men and women concerned only with profit and their own pleasures deeply offends God.

As we have seen (p. 83), the Old Testament Law made careful and explicit provision to meet the needs of *all* His people. When a man sold himself or one of his family into servitude, it was *not slavery*. He would be released later and restored to his ancestral land (Lev. 25). Widows and others without means of support were provided for. Each farmer was to allow gleaning, the gathering of part of his harvest by the poor. All grain that fell to the ground was to be left for the poor. Fruit of the vine and tree was not to be completely harvested by the owner. There was no welfare roll in Israel; the poor maintained their self-respect and worked for what they received. The man who had plenty made the excess available to the less fortunate. No wonder the Old Testament promised that, should Israel obey God's Law, "there shall be no poor among you" (Deut. 15:4, 5)!

God's Law was a charter for a truly just society.

Those laws, and God Himself, were now being denied by His people. Love for neighbor and respect for the poor had been long forgotten. In their place had come deep social cleavage; brutal oppression was undertaken for material gain.

Justice. Significant also is the insight Amos gives us into the nature of justice and righteousness. Too often we think of these qualities as related to rules of behavior—to what a person does or does not do.

Amos, reflecting the Old Testament Law, focuses our attention on God's concern for people. The purpose behind the laws governing society takes on crucial importance. The laws were given that each person, rich and poor alike, might be treated with fairness and compassion. In essence, Amos helps us see that the concept of God being just is in fact an affirmation that God is committed to do right by all men. What is more, God's own deep commitment to

85

justice leads Him to require that in human society we also maintain a commitment to do right by all.

Ritual. The thrust of Amos's message is the announcement of God's judgment on Israel for their injustice.

Israel had never turned away from the worship centers erected by Jeroboam I. She still bowed down to golden calves. What is more, Baal worship had again crept into the land. Altars were again built on high ridges of land in honor of the ancient nature gods, and around them the old immoralities were practiced still—in the name of religion.

The ritual, even when performed in God's supposed honor, horrified Him.

> Because I know your transgressions are many
>   and your sins are great,
> You who distress the righteous and accept
>   bribes,
> And turn aside the poor in the gate.
>
> *Amos 5:12*

God's demand focused not on restoring the appropriate forms of worship, but on returning again to His values and sharing His own commitment to do right by all.

> Seek good and not evil, that you may live;
> And thus may the Lord God of hosts be with
>   you,
> Just as you have said!
> Hate evil, love good,

And establish justice in the gate!
Perhaps the Lord God of hosts
May be gracious to the remnant of Joseph.

Amos 5:14, 15

It is the heart of man with which God is concerned. In turning away from God, Israel lost touch with the divine values. Rejecting righteousness and justice, God's people abandoned themselves to wealth and pleasure and to oppression of the poor.

And to punishment.

Israel had passed beyond the edge of judgment.

GOING DEEPER

to personalize

1. Read the Book of Amos, underlining passages which give you insight into the moral, social, economic, and spiritual conditions of Amos's day.

2. The Book of Amos gives us important insight into the character and personality of God. What qualities do you see in such verses as 3:7; 4:2, 6-11, 13; 5:4, 6, 8, 21, 22; 6:8; 7:2, 3, 5; 9:2-4, 7? Write a one-page portrait of God based on Amos.

3. Outlining is a key method of Bible study. Page 81 contains an overall outline of Amos. Take one of the following sections and do a *detailed* outline of its content: Amos 3:1-15; 4:1-13; 5:1—6:14.

4. Justice is clearly a thing of great important to God. (Note: *justice* and *righteousness* are both translations of the same Hebrew word in the Old Testament.) How would you define *justice* as Amos por-

trays it?

5. What parallels can you see between Amos's society and our own? Develop a thorough list—and be prepared to discuss: Does Amos's message apply to us today? If so, how?

to probe

1. From the Old Testament Law (especially in Exodus, Leviticus, and Deuteronomy) describe the just society.

2. Study what the Bible says about the poor. Either use a concordance study for the whole Bible or limit your study to Proverbs. What does your study reveal that is relevant to our society today? Do you see any guidelines or principles to help us face our problems with oppression and poverty?

REVIVAL

WHEN SOLOMON'S KINGDOM WAS TORN in 931 B.C., the Southern Kingdom, Judah, comprised considerably less territory and had a much smaller population. In the initial years of conflict between the two kingdoms, however, many from Israel drifted across the border. Committed to the worship of Jehovah, they remained faithful to the Jerusalem Temple and to the festivals that God had instituted through Moses. They rejected Bethel and Dan and the counterfeit priesthood ordained by Jeroboam I.

But as the decades passed, the once-united nation accepted its divided state. And any initial claim of Judah to a special godliness was lost.

Of Judah's nineteen kings, Scripture marks out eight as "good." Characteristically, these kings stimulated revivals. Yet the fact that the Southern Kingdom even needed revival, plus the Bible's description of the sins that were put away, tells us that

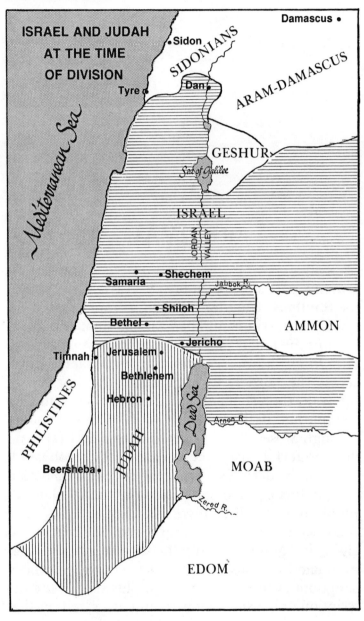

ISRAEL AND JUDAH
AT THE TIME
OF DIVISION

Mediterranean Sea

Damascus •

• Sidon

SIDONIANS

ARAM-DAMASCUS

Tyre •

Dan •

GESHUR

Sea of Galilee

ISRAEL

JORDAN VALLEY

• Shechem

Samaria •

Jabbok R.

• Shiloh

Bethel •

AMMON

• Jericho

Timnah •

Jerusalem •

Bethlehem •

Dead Sea

Hebron •

Arnon R.

PHILISTINES

Beersheba •

JUDAH

MOAB

Zered R.

EDOM

90

Judah tended to fall into the same apostasy that plagued Israel.

Asa (2 Chron. 14, 15) removed idols from the land as well as the male prostitutes associated with their worship. He also deposed his grandmother as queen mother because she had made an idol to Asherah. Encouraged by the prophet Azariah, Asa led Judah to renew their covenant promises to God.

Yet Asa did not remain committed to God. In his later years, he imprisoned the prophet Hanani for rebuking him, and he failed to turn to God for aid when he was ill (2 Chron. 16).

Jehoshaphat, Asa's son, also followed the Lord. Like Asa, he attempted to root out the worship of Baal and removed many "high places." These high places *(bamoth)* were elevations set aside for pagan worship. Each contained an altar featuring idols. Sometimes the Hebrews would set aside a high place for the worship of the Lord and ordain local priests. This practice was in direct violation of the Old Testament Law, which insisted on a single center for worship and sacrifice (Jerusalem during the kingdom years) and on a priesthood composed of descendants of Aaron, Moses' brother. The pagan associations of the high places were much too strong; worship there would soon take on the characteristics of occultism and immorality.

So Jehoshaphat's attack on the high places was undertaken out of zeal for God, as was his insistence that the Levites resume their ministry of traveling to teach the "book of the Law" throughout Judah (2 Chron. 17:9).

91

The next kings of Judah were evil, and set an example gladly followed by the people. Strangely, Athaliah, a daughter of Jezebel (the wife of Israel's King Ahab), actually came to reign in Judah and aggressively promoted the cult of Baal.

However, there was a core of godly resistance to Athaliah. After six years, Jehoiada, the high priest, secretly crowned seven-year-old Joash as king. The boy had been hidden six years from Athaliah, who had had all other possible claimants to the throne executed. Now military and religious leaders combined to bring about the coup, and Athaliah was quickly executed (2 Chron. 22:10—23:15).

Joash and the four kings who followed him were relatively good kings. Under Joash, the priests of Baal were killed and the pagan altars and idols destroyed. The Temple was repaired and worship of God reinstituted. But in Joash's later years, he also faltered. After the high priest who had crowned and advised him died, Joash turned aside from God.

Under the later kings, Judah knew both trial and triumph. As in the Northern Kingdom, increasing prosperity led to the neglect of faith. Ahaz, Judah's king during the years preceding the destruction of Samaria, committed himself to evil. He promoted the worship of Baal and even engaged in infant sacrifice (2 Chron. 28:3). He also established a pagan altar in the Jerusalem Temple as the official place of sacrifice and finally closed the Temple to force his people into the way of worship that he wanted. Micah, a contemporary prophet, cried out against Judah in the days before Israel's destruction:

The statues of Omri
And all the works of the house of Ahab are
   observed:
And in their devices you walk.
Therefore, I will give you up for destruction
And your inhabitants for derision,
And you will bear the reproach of My people.
Micah 6:16

How little difference could be seen between the sins of the Northern Kingdom and the life-style of "godly" Judah! Much later, as the destruction Micah foretold actually struck, Jeremiah looked back on the captivity of the Northern Kingdom as a special lesson to Judah—a unique call to revival. The words God communicated to Jeremiah clearly indicate that all the revivals of the Southern Kingdom, even the greatest under Hezekiah and Josiah, had not touched the hearts of God's chosen.

"Have you seen what faithless Israel did?" said the Lord. "She went up on every high hill and under every green tree, and she was a harlot there. And I thought, 'After she has done these things, she will return to me'; but she did not return, and her treacherous sister Judah saw it. And I saw that for all the adulteries of faithless Israel, I had sent her away and given her a writ of divorce, yet her treacherous sister Judah did not fear; but she went and was a harlot also. And it came about because of the lightness of her harlotry, that she polluted the land and committed adultery with stones and trees. And yet in spite of all this her treacherous sister Judah did not return to Me with all her heart, but rather in deception," declares the Lord.

Jeremiah 3:6-10

In Judah, the outward forms of religion were correct. But the hearts of the people had drifted as far from God as had the hearts of the men of Israel.

JOEL

By 830 B.C., the date most conservative scholars set for the ministry of Joel, the pattern of revival and decline in Judah had become clear. Just as Jonah's book communicated a basic message to the North—a message promising a second chance if they would return to God—so does the Book of Joel contain a basic message to Judah. Through the decades of ups and downs, of revival and apostasy, the words of Joel would echo in the ears of a "religious" people as a call for *wholehearted* return. Superficial reform or ritual revivals could never bring the blessing that would follow true revival. Listen to Joel's words:

> "Yet even now," declares the Lord,
> "Return to Me with all your heart,
> And with fasting, weeping, and mourning;
> And rend your heart and not your garments."
> Now return to the Lord your God,
> For He is gracious and compassionate,

Slow to anger, abounding in lovingkindness,
And relenting of evil
Who knows whether He will not run and relent,
And leave a blessing behind Him,
Even a grain offering and a libation
For the Lord your God?
Blow a trumpet in Zion,
Consecrate a fast, proclaim a solemn assembly,
Gather the people, sanctify the congregation,
Assemble the elders,
Gather the children and the nursing infants.
Let the bridegroom come out of his room
And the bride out of her bridal chamber.
Let the priests, the Lord's ministers,
Weep between the porch and the altar,
And let them say, "Spare Thy people, O Lord,
And do not make Thine inheritance a re-
    proach,
A byword among the nations,"
Why should they among peoples say,
"Where is their God?"

Then the Lord will be zealous for His land,
And will have pity on His people.

Joel 2:12-18

Joel's message breaks naturally into two sections. The first section, 1:2—2:17, are words of the prophet himself.

Apparently a series of calamities, especially a great swarm of locusts, had struck Judah. Joel looked on this insect horde as the forerunner of

95

even more terrible punishments unless God's people came to genuine repentance. Both the locusts and the human enemy they may have foreshadowed were recognized by Joel as being led by Jehovah Himself. Only destruction could follow should God's people waver between holiness and evil, between the Lord and the sensual pagan gods of Canaan.

The second section of Joel's message (2:18—3:21) gives the response of Jehovah. God promised that after His people returned to Him "with all your heart" they would know the fullness of blessing promised under the ancient Abrahamic Covenant. The land would overflow with its produce (2:19, 21-16; 3:18). Israel's enemies would be overcome (2:20; 3:1-17, 19-20). God Himself would be among His people in a unique way (2:27), and they would be regathered from the lands in which they had been scattered (3:5-7). Great spiritual blessing would be poured out on all mankind as a consequence of the return of God's people to Him (2:28-32).

The message of Joel's has a very clear pattern:
- *Calamities are God's warning of judgment to come.*
- *Heed the warnings, and return with all your heart.*
- *When you return, God's fullest blessing will be poured out on you and all people.*

Judah, which had become a land of superficial religion, had in Joel's prophecy a basic message that would be reflected in the ministry of each later prophet God would send. But the revivals that did follow would never penetrate to the heart commitment of the people of that land. Like her sister kingdom to the north, Judah would appear at public worship and pretend ... only to slip away afterward to the high places and there be unfaithful to her God.

PREDICTIVE PROPHECY

There are elements of Joel's prophecy which modern scholars study and firmly believe refer to events still future to our own day. Very often Old Testament books are studied solely to isolate their indications of the future, and rigid eschatological systems are constructed.

There *is* a still-future dimension to many Old Testament writings. In some prophetic books, large sections are specifically devoted to pictures of the future. This is why in the final book of our Old Testament study series, *Springtime Coming*, we will look at the major Old Testament themes about the future and find an exciting sketch of God's plan for the days yet ahead.

But when reading an Old Testament prophet such as Joel or Amos, it is important to realize that *each prophet was presenting a message for his own time.* Joel and the rest were God's spokesmen to a living people; each message was shaped to its own historical setting and conditions. Whatever picture Joel may give of the future, we need to concentrate on the book's purpose *in that historical setting* to understand its basic message and its meaning for us today. So, setting aside for the time being any fascinating speculations about our future, we want to concentrate on what the prophets said to people of their time, and in view of that meaning to discern the message God has for us today.

With Joel, each message is clear. Superficial religion and a divided heart can never satisfy God. Any revival that substitutes emotionalism, with repeated altar calls and repeated failures, is no pattern for our relationship with God. To know God and to be His people calls for commitment.

Christ's invitation in the gospel is not just to return, but to return with all your heart. Complete commitment is the unchanging avenue to blessing.

GOING DEEPER

to personalize

1. To get a picture of the experience of the Southern Kingdom before 722, read 2 Chronicles 10—28.

2. Read Joel.

3. Then *either:*

a. Develop a chart on which you compare and contrast features of the revivals under Asa, Jehoshaphat, and Joash;

b. Or do a careful outline of the Book of Joel;

c. Or write a song to communicate the basic message of Joel.

to probe

1. Expand the chart (3a, above) to include comparisons of revivals under Hezekiah (2 Chron. 29—32) and Josiah (2 Chron. 34, 35).

2. Imagine yourself to be a Hebrew of Joel's day. Write a letter to a friend telling about Joel's message. Interpret the message to your friend, making special reference to the last one hundred years of Judah's and Israel's history. Do a careful job, at least five to eight pages long.

"WE'RE RIGHT!"

IT HAS ALWAYS BEEN A GREAT TEMPTATION for the true believer to rely on his orthodoxy.

We see it in our own time. In a New Mexico church a young ministerial intern found his marriage hurting. His wife left and returned to her parents' home. The pastor called the young man in, and rather than offering support and help to repair the broken relationship, demanded his resignation. Unsatisfied by the letter of resignation that was submitted, the pastor rewrote the letter and sent his version out to the congregation over the young man's signature. He then insisted the intern simply disappear; there would be no farewells or good-bye gatherings.

When the people began to probe and ask why they had not had a chance to express appreciation for the young man's ministry, the pastor held an exorcism in the church, banning the devil who was manifesting himself in the "critical spirit" of the people!

Although this pastor's actions showed a total and calloused disregard for the deep need and pain of the young couple, he could always justify his action on the ground that he was "right."

The Pharisees operated on this same principle. Jesus was criticized—not for His miracles of compassion and healing, not for His capacity to touch unresponsive people and bring them into relationship with God—but because He did not wash His hands the way the Pharisees thought was "right," or because His disciples disregarded a tradition of men (not a word from God) and plucked ears of grain to eat as they walked through a field on the Sabbath. To the Pharisees, being "right" was an excuse to justify any and all comment, however unloving it might be.

We need to remember this tendency of the religious to justify themselves when we look at the Book of Micah. For Micah gives a prophetic warning—not to wayward Israel but to orthodox Judah.

BACKGROUND

Micah was a contemporary of Isaiah (whose book we explore in depth in *Lift High the Torch,* another of this Old Testament survey series). He and Isaiah both prophesied to Judah, the Southern Kingdom, at the time when Israel was carried into captivity by the Assyrian king, Sargon II. Most date Micah's ministry from around 730 to 700 B.C.

These were tense days for Judah. Even though

101

led by godly King Hezekiah, who worked wholeheartedly to bring revival, the Assyrian menace constantly loomed over little Judah.

As was characteristic, Hezekiah's ministry brought a form of revival, but it was superficial; it did not touch the hearts of the people. Yet the combined ministry of these three godly men—Micah, Isaiah, and Hezekiah—was used by God to pull His people away from the edge of judgment. The Assyrians did indeed invade Judah. Following Sargon's death, Sennacherib captured some forty-six Judean cities (including most of those spoken of by Micah in chapter 1), and according to Assyrian records shut up Hezekiah in Jerusalem "like a bird in a cage."

But the city itself was delivered. Despite the continuing threat, God protected the remnant of His people. The incipient sin we see portrayed in the Books of Isaiah and of Micah had not yet matured. God would hold off judgment; His people would have yet another chance.

Being "right." It is clear that even under the preaching of Micah and Isaiah the mass of Judah's population still did not grasp the reality of their situation. Hezekiah had initiated great religious reforms. Most people assumed that this ritual reformation was what had protected them from their enemies.

This was one illusion the people of the Northern Kingdom had never had.

The Northern Kingdom was founded with a false religious system, with counterfeit worship centers at Bethel and Dan, where counterfeit priests offered counterfeit sacrifices before counterfeit gods on counterfeit holy days. The whole ritual of the nation's official faith was *wrong*. Yet even this unorthodox approach to Jehovah worship was not the dominant faith in the days of the Assyrian invasion. It was the worship of Baal and Asherah, with pagan excesses committed on every height of ground, which gave abundant testimony to Israel's religious apostasy.

The social evils, the materialism, and the oppression which marked the society of the Northern Kingdom merely demonstrated the departure from God to which Israel's religion blatantly testified.

With the reforms instituted by Hezekiah, Judah's religious observances could not be faulted. Her official faith—or state religion, if you will—was beautifully orthodox. The House of God had been cleansed, the priests sanctified for ministry. Jerusalem altars erected to heathen deities were destroyed and the commanded feasts and sacrifices kept. The ways of praise instituted by David were restored; the psalms were again sung. Throughout Judah and Ephraim and Manasseh the pillars and altars to Baal were crushed and burned. The orthodox faith of the Old Testament was scrupulously observed, and Judah took great comfort in the notion that her faith was "right."

The heart. Micah does not seem to have been impressed. Looking beneath the externals of ritual and form, Micah evaluated the heart of God's people and found it as perverse and ungodly as the heart of the men of the North.

103

> Now hear this, heads of the house of Jacob
> And rulers of the house of Israel. . . .
> Who build Zion with bloodshed
> And Jerusalem with violent injustice.
> Her leaders pronounce judgment for a bribe,
> Her priests instruct for a price,
> And her prophets divine for money.
> Yet they lean on the Lord, saying,
> "Is not the Lord in our midst?
> Calamity will not come upon us."
>
> *Micah 3:9-11*

Judah was placing its confidence in the outward orthodoxy of its ritual—just as many of us today place our confidence in the orthodoxy of our doctrine. But God demands more.

Micah, in words that seem to echo Amos's message to the people of the Northern Kingdom, urges a return to God that will be demonstrated in a change of heart—a change of heart that will necessarily issue in a life-style of love and justice, of compassion and caring for our fellowmen as we walk close to God.

> With what shall I come to the Lord
> And bow myself before the God on high?
> Shall I come to Him with burnt offerings,
> With yearling calves?
> Does the Lord take delight in thousands of
>   rams,
> In ten thousand rivers of oil?
> Shall I present my first-born for my rebellious
>   acts,

The fruit of my body for the sin of my soul?
He has told you, O man, what is good;
And what does the Lord require of you
But to do justice, to love kindness,
And to walk humbly with your God?

Micah 6:6-8

Orthodoxy is never enough. Being right with God will be expressed in godly and compassionate living.

In a very real way, Micah is a book that speaks directly to us in our day. We are "right" in our doctrine. We are "right" in much of our practice. But our orthodoxy is an empty shell, a basis for even greater judgment, unless God's truth has warmed our hearts and moved us into relationships with individuals and with society in which we do justice, love kindness, and walk humbly with our God.

MICAH'S MESSAGE

Seen in the context of its time, Micah's message takes on special significance. We can see the structure of the book and message by tracing the following outline.

THE BOOK OF MICAH

I. Immediate national judgment coming
  A. Judgment announced   1:2-5
  B. Judgment described   1:6-8
  C. Judgment explained
    1. As amputation of a diseased limb   1:9-16
    2. As redressing of injustice   2:1-13

105

Reading through Micah, guided by our outline, let's trace the thoughts of this significant book.

Micah, identified in 1:1 as a prophet who ministered in the reigns of Jotham, Ahaz, and Hezekiah, launches immediately into his message concerning Samaria and Jerusalem.

1:2-5. Judgment is announced, as God is seen stepping out from His holy Temple. To God, both Samaria, the capital of the Northern Kingdom, and Jerusalem, capital and site of the Temple in the South, are identified as rebellious high places.

1:9–2:13. The explanation of the judgment is given under two figures. The first is a graphic analogy (1:9-16). Samaria's idolatry and rebellion are likened to a wound which will not heal. Instead, the wound fills with pus, and infection and inflammation spread. Finally, there is no recourse but to amputate the wounded limb and all the surrounding body that has been infected. According to Micah's description, the infection has spread to reach "the gate of my people, even to Jerusalem" (v. 9). When the Assyrians come, the cities between the Northern Kingdom and Jerusalem will be taken, too, "because in you were found the rebellious acts of Israel" (v. 13).

The second picture seems to imply a set of balances (2:1-13). There is a point and counterpoint structure to the passage:

sin described	balancing judgment
2:1, 2	2:3-5
2:6-11	2:12, 13

First, as in Amos, God focuses attention on Judah's injustice, describing men who lie awake scheming to defraud their neighbors. Therefore, God says (2:3), calamity will come upon the family of Judah, and the fields the oppressors plotted to gain will be distributed to "apostates"—to a pagan people whom the victorious Assyrians would resettle in Israel.

Second, Micah speaks of the reaction of the people to his prophetic ministry. They say, "Do not speak out" (v. 6) . . . and then they speak out with their own version of God's message. And this from people who "strip the robe off a fellow-Israelite" (v. 8) and evict widows! They are ready to listen to a drunkard, but they will not hear the Word of the Lord. The result? God must balance their sin with judgment:

I will surely assemble all of you, Jacob,
I will surely gather the remnant of Israel.

Micah 2:12

107

Then, gathered together in the midst of their pastures, God Himself will lead a robber band to break in and to drag them out and away.

God *is* just; His holiness demands that the sin of His people be balanced by judgment.

With the immediate fate described and justified, Micah turns to a restatement of principles found earlier in God's Word. While God has committed Himself as a holy God to punish sin, He has also committed Himself to the ultimate good and blessing of His people.

3:1-12. Graphically, Micah reviews the sins that mar the life-style of God's people. He pictures their injustice as a brutal cannibalism (3:2, 3) in which the very life of the poor is torn from them. He sketches the prophets as gross gluttons, always willing to cry "Peace" and promise good news if their mouths are filled, but who are enemies of those "who put nothing in their mouths" (v. 5). Gluttony, not God, is the source of their messages. Their leaders take bribes, the city is filled with violence, and yet because of the presence of the Temple where their empty rituals are repeated, they "lean upon the Lord" (v. 11). The Temple, polluted by their sins, will one day lie in ruin—and their empty hopes with it. God's holiness remains unchanged; sin *will* be judged.

4:1-5. When the judgment comes, it must not be interpreted as total repudiation. Looking ahead to the end of history, Micah conveys God's promise that the whole world will come to Jerusalem to learn of God and His ways, and that in those days God Himself will rule. Implements of war will be reshaped to harvest the bounty of the earth, and all men will live in peace and plenty.

Whatever comes, God will preserve a remnant of His people so that the time of promised blessing may be assured.

4:9–5:1. But the present is to be a time of agony when Judah will be displaced. The exile of Judah will not be at the hands of Assyria, but of Babylon (4:10). From Babylon, God's people will be regathered.

Scattering and regathering, scattering and regathering—this is the pattern of judgment which Israel and Judah will experience until God finally brings all His promises to pass.

5:2-15. At this point, Micah introduces the Messiah—the promised One on whose coming all the plans and purposes of God hinge. He will be born as a man in Bethlehem (5:2), even though "his goings forth are . . . from the days of eternity." When Messiah comes, He will shepherd His people, deliver the scattered remnant, destroy Israel's enemies, and change the heart of God's people to root out all that has been associated with their sin.

Most of the Old Testament deals with the national experience of God's people. Judgments are announced upon the Hebrew people; promises tell of national restoration. The corporate responsiveness or unresponsiveness of the nation as a whole is clearly the basis of God's dealing with His people.

Often the question is raised: What about the individual? Didn't God care about individuals in Old

Testament days? Was the godly person swallowed up in judgments against the majority?

Micah helps us to answer such questions and to see that throughout history God has retained concern for the individual. In every age, God's overall working in history and society harmonizes with His love of each person.

What, then, does God say to the individual who lives in an unjust society and whose experience is shaped by environment?

6:1-5. The message to individuals begins with a plea to realize that God *does* have a valid case against Israel. God brought His people out of Egypt, ransomed them, gave leaders to guide them, protected and guarded them that they might "know the righteous acts of the Lord" (v. 5), i.e., that they might obey and experience all the good things which God would then be free to shower upon them. But Israel had turned away, bored with God and His ways.

The righteous person will see the situation from God's perspective, even when the judgment brings him personal affliction.

6:6-8. What can the individual who recognizes the righteousness of God's cause do? "He has told you, O man, what is good; and what does the Lord require of you but to do justice, to love kindness, and walk humbly with your God?" (v. 8).

6:9-7:6. Reviewing again the sins of the society in which the just live, God points out that He *must* act to judge it. "Can I justify wicked scales and a bag of deceptive weights?" (6:11). No, punishment must come. And when it does, the just in that society must

110

undergo the same experiences as the unjust.

7:7-20. How then is the believer to respond in times of judgment? Micah gives two answers.

First (vv. 7-13), suffering in such a time is to be expected. It is just. The individual *does* bear responsibility for his society (v. 9). Yet during such a time of discipline the true believer will not lose hope in God: "Though I fall I will rise; though I dwell in darkness, the Lord is a light for me" (v. 8).

Second (vv. 14-20), the believer takes comfort in his confidence in God's commitment to bring him good in the end. We think in terms of eternity; the godly Jew characteristically thought of a national restoration. In either case, God *will* do what He intends and bring us everlasting good. The sufferings of this time are not fit to be compared with the glory to come. So Micah concludes:

> Who is God like Thee, who pardons iniquity
> And passes over the rebellious act of the
>   remnant of His possession?
> He does not retain His anger forever,
> Because He delights in unchanging love.
> He will again have compassion on us;
> He will tread our iniquities underfoot.
> Yes, Thou wilt cast all their sins
> Into the depths of the sea.
> Thou wilt give truth to Jacob
> And unchanging love to Abraham
> Which Thou didst swear to our forefathers
> From the days of old.
>
> *Micah 7:18-20*

111

GOING DEEPER

to personalize

1. Read the historical background sketching the time in which Micah ministered: 2 Chron. 28-32.

2. Read Micah, following the outline (and, if you wish, the notes in the text, pp. 105-111).

3. There are several word pictures in Micah which communicate graphically God's view of the situation in Israel and Judah and what He will do to remedy it. Among them are the pictures of the wound (1: 9-16), the men who lie awake plotting oppression (2: 1, 2), "cannibalism" (3: 2, 3), etc. Read the book to find as many of these word pictures as you can. Draw cartoons of three of them.

4. What application can you see of Micah's message to our day? Whom do you think would be identified by God as those who insist they are "right" but lack God's heart for others? What would He say to them today? How is our society—or our churches—like Judah? Think this one through, and jot down your thoughts.

5. Merton Strommen did a study of young people and their values and concluded that there was no significant difference in values between churched and unchurched teens. Do you think this is significant? Why, or why not?

to probe

Isaiah and Micah were contemporaries. Compare the following common elements in their messages:

Micah	*Isaiah*
1:9-16	10:28-32
2:1, 2	5:8
2:6, 11	30:10
2:12	10:20-23
3:5-7	29:9-12
4:1	2:2
4:4	1:19
4:7	9:7
5:2-4	7:14
4:10	39:6
5:6	14:25
6:6-8	58:6, 7
7:7	8:17
7:12	11:11

9

Jeremiah 1-20, 22, 23, 25, 26, 35, 36, 45-48

BEGINNING OF THE END

THE REIGN OF MANASSEH was the beginning of the end for Judah.

The Southern Kingdom, though threatened, survived the Assyrian invasion and had a religious as well as political resurgence under Hezekiah. But Manasseh, Hezekiah's son, plunged Judah into the same kind of idolatry that the Northern Kingdom had known under Ahab and Jezebel. The Temple was polluted with pagan altars, the occult was promoted by the king, and child sacrifice to Moloch was practiced in the Hinnom Valley near Jerusalem.

Tradition tells us that Isaiah spoke out against the king and was executed, as were many other pious leaders who dared to protest (2 Kings 21:16).

Manasseh's forty-four-year reign did not bring prosperity to Judah. In 678 B.C., he and twenty-one other kings made a compulsory visit to swear allegiance to Assyria. Later Manasseh apparently involved Judah in a rebellion of Moab and Edom against Assyrian control and was taken prisoner to Babylon. There, the Bible tells us, Manasseh "humbled himself greatly before the God of his fathers" and was returned to Judah by the Assyrians. "Then," adds the text, "Manasseh knew that the Lord was God" (2 Chron. 33:10-13). Following his release, Manasseh attempted to institute his own revival. He cleansed the Temple, threw down the centers of idolatry in Jerusalem, and "ordered Judah to serve the Lord God of Israel" (2 Chron. 33:16).

But the people did not respond. Judah, too, had passed beyond the edge of judgment, and destruction was sure to come.

Jeremiah. Jeremiah was born about 648 B.C. and grew up as a contemporary of Manasseh's grandson, Josiah. Living only about two miles from Jerusalem and coming from a priestly family, he would have been intimately acquainted with the political situation in Judah.

At age twenty, in 627 B.C., God told Jeremiah that he was to be His prophet. Jeremiah objected that he was too young, but God answered:

> Do not say, "I am a youth."
> Because everywhere I send you, you shall go,
> And all that I command you, you shall speak.
> Do not be afraid of them,
> For I am with you to deliver you.
> *Jeremiah 1:7, 8*

115

Thus commanded, Jeremiah was told that His ministry would be one of judgment and punishment, but would also bring a unique recovery of hope:

> See, I have appointed you this day over the
>   nations and over the kingdoms,
> To pluck up and to break down,
> To destroy and to overthrow,
> To build and to plant.
>
> *Jeremiah 1:10*

This call set the tone for Jeremiah's long life. Obeying his call, he urged his countrymen to surrender to Babylon, whom God showed him to be the instrument of His chastisement. Such a demand could be viewed only as treason. So Jeremiah was imprisoned, his life threatened, and his ministry constantly rejected by God's people.

Jeremiah lived and ministered under a succession of kings: first, godly King Josiah, and then a series of ungodly rulers: Jehoiakim, Zedekiah, and Gedaliah. His book can best be understood and the progress of the times viewed if the various messages and sermons are organized according to the king in whose reign each was spoken.

In this chapter and in the one to follow, we will look through the eyes of Jeremiah at the last days of the surviving kingdom and trace in his words the final sins which brought on the Babylonian Captivity.

JEREMIAH'S MINISTRY UNDER JOSIAH
626–609 B.C.

Josiah was eight years old when he became king.
At sixteen, he began to seek God, and by twenty, he
initiated a vigorous religious revival. The idols in-
troduced by Manasseh were purged, and Josiah ven-
tured out into the countryside to cleanse the whole
land.

JEREMIAH'S TIMES*

686—Manasseh becomes sole king
648—Josiah born
642—Amon succeeds Manasseh as king
640—Josiah becomes king
633—Josiah at 16 seeks after God
628—Josiah at 20 begins reforms
627—Jeremiah at 20 called as prophet
621—Mosaic Law found in Temple
612—Nineveh destroyed as Nahum prophesied
609—Josiah slain in battle at Megiddo; Jehoiakim becomes king
605—Babylon defeats Egypt at Carchemish; Daniel, other hos-
    tages taken to Babylon (Dan. 1:1); Nebuchadnezzar be-
    comes king of Babylon
604—Nebuchadnezzar receives tribute in Palestine
601—Nebuchadnezzar defeated near Egypt
598—Jehoiakim set aside; Jehoiachin rules from Dec. 9 to
    March 16, 597, is then deported April 22 to Babylon
597—Zedekiah becomes king in Judah
588—Babylon lays siege to Jerusalem on Jan. 15
587—Jeremiah imprisoned (Jer. 32:1, 2)
586— Zedekiah flees July 18; destruction of city begins Aug. 14;
    Gedaliah killed and Jews migrate to Egypt against God's
    command Oct. 7

*Adapted from the *Zondervan Pictorial Bible Encyclopedia*, Vol. 3, p. 435.

This four-year project completed, Josiah set about repairing the Temple in Jerusalem and, as had happened in an earlier day, the lost books of Moses were again recovered. When the books were read, Josiah was horrified to discover the curses God had placed on the very life-style that Judah had adopted (Deut. 28:15-68), and he set about immediately to find out what God intended. Asking the prophetess Huldah, the king was informed that all the judgments surely would come upon Judah, but that because of his own relationship with God the days of his reign would be peaceful.

Relieved, and more than ever committed to the Lord, Josiah gathered all the people to hear the words of God's book read aloud. He himself renewed the Covenant with God, promising to respond and keep God's words with all his heart. And 2 Chronicles 34:32 tells us that Josiah caused ("made"!) all present in Jerusalem make the same promises.

Thus, under Josiah, the ancient feasts and worship were reinstituted. Thus, too, Habakkuk, the troubled Levite we met at the beginning of our study, came to Jerusalem and took a leading role in the revival of worship.

But Habakkuk had been a worried, deeply concerned man. In spite of the outward signs of revival under Josiah, Habakkuk sensed the deep-seated evil which still revealed itself on the hills of Judah and in the injustice which marked the society.

Reading Jeremiah's messages, we can see more clearly why Habakkuk was troubled. Very likely he

JEREMIAH'S MESSAGES DURING JOSIAH'S REIGN	
2:1—3:5	Judah's sinful heart
3:6—6:30	Jerusalem to be destroyed
7:1—10:25	Ruin and exile coming
18:1—20:18	Message on the potter

heard Jeremiah speak, saw the sins he pointed out, and in a godly response to the message of God's Word came to see Judah from the divine perspective. What, then, would Habakkuk have heard as Jeremiah ministered during the days of Judah's last revival?

Jer. 2:1–3:5. Jeremiah denounced Judah's sin in defiling the land with Baals and other false gods. "My people have committed two evils," Jeremiah cried as God's spokesman. "They have forsaken Me, the fountain of living waters, to hew for themselves cisterns, broken cisterns, that can hold no water" (2:13).

Jer. 3:6–6:30. This impassioned appeal by Jeremiah to return to God supported Josiah's attempt at revival. Promising a "pleasant land," Jeremiah, in God's name, begged His people to return and "only acknowledge your iniquity" (3:13). Unless there would be such a return, Jeremiah could envision only one future:

> I looked on the mountains, and behold, they
>   were quaking,
> And all the hills moved to and fro.
> I looked, and behold, there was no man,

119

And all the birds of the heavens had fled.
I looked, and behold, the fruitful land was a
    wilderness,
And all its cities were pulled down
Before the Lord, before His fierce anger.

Jeremiah 4:24-26

Jer. 7:1–10:25. As the outward signs of return to God began to be seen in the restored Temple, Jeremiah stood in its gates and warned against trust in ritual.

"Amend your ways and your deeds," the spokesman cried, "and I will let you dwell in this place. Do not trust in deceptive words, saying, 'This is the temple of the Lord, the temple of the Lord, the temple of the Lord.' For if you truly amend your ways and your deeds, if you truly practice justice between a man and his neighbor, if you do not oppress the alien, the orphan, or the widow, and do not shed innocent blood in this place, nor walk after other gods to your own ruin, then I will let you dwell in this place" (7:4-7). Again, the choice Judah must make is fully explained and the consequence examined. If there is no response to "the Lord who exercises lovingkindness, justice, and righteousness on earth" (9:24), then surely Judah will be dragged away into captivity.

Jer. 18:1–20:18. This last message associated with the days of Josiah reflects the prophet's growing awareness that Judah *has* made her choice. Whatever God warns or commands, only one response can be expected: "But they will say, 'It's hopeless! For we are going to follow our own plans, and each of us will act according to the stubbornness of his evil heart' " (18:12).

Watching a potter shape a clay pot on his wheel, Jeremiah sees a vessel spoiled—and the clay remade into another vessel. Unresponsive Israel has not obeyed: now it must become a formless lump which later *will* respond to the potter's hand. Taking a pottery bowl, Jeremiah is sent to confront the leaders and inhabitants of Jerusalem. He breaks the jar before them and informs them that God has determined to break the city in just the same way, for it, too, is beyond repair.

When the chief priest hears of Jeremiah's words, he has the prophet beaten and put in stocks as a humiliating punishment. Eventually released, Jeremiah defiantly announces destruction on both city and priest.

But the last verses of this chapter help us see how much the prophet himself suffered in his rejection. Very probably these words also reflect his deep despair, for the godly King Josiah had recently been killed in battle. When Josiah fell, Jeremiah's hope was also destroyed. The full realization that he must live through the last days of the surviving kingdom, prophesying warnings to a people who would not listen, must have come home with stunning force.

No wonder the mourning prophet's feelings burst out in agonized expression:

Cursed be the day when I was born;

121

Let the day not be blessed when my mother
  bore me!
Cursed be the man who brought the news
To my father, saying,
"A baby boy has been born to you!"
And made him very happy.
But let that man be like the cities
Which the Lord overthrew without relenting,
And let him hear an outcry in the morning
And a shout of alarm at noon;
Because he did not kill me before birth,
So that my mother would have been my grave,
And her womb ever pregnant.
Why did I ever come forth from the womb
To look on trouble and sorrow,
So that my days have been spent in shame?
Jeremiah 20:14-18

JEREMIAH'S MINISTRY UNDER JEHOIAKIM
609–598 B.C.

In the fourth year of Jehoiakim's reign, Nebuchadnezzar defeated the Egyptians in the Battle of Carchemish, firmly establishing the Babylonians as the dominant world power. Hostages were taken by the victorious Nebuchadnezzar, whom Jeremiah identified as the servant God had chosen to judge Judah and the other nations of Palestine. He predicted a great captivity, to last seventy years, and at God's instructions made a written record of his sermons and messages.

This scroll fell into the hands of King Jehoiakim,

JEREMIAH'S MESSAGES DURING JEHOIAKIM'S REIGN	
11:1—13:14	The broken covenant
chs. 14, 15	Prayers are fruitless
chs. 16, 17	Jeremiah's celibacy
ch. 22	The king rejected
ch. 23	False prophets charged
ch. 25	Nebuchadnezzar is God's servant
ch. 26	Jeremiah threatened with death
ch. 35	Example of the Rechabites
ch. 36	Various warnings
ch. 45	Promise to Baruch
chs. 46—48	Against foreign nations

who ordered it burnt and commanded the arrest of the prophet and his secretary, Baruch. Even under arrest, Jeremiah continued the dire prophecy which God commanded, adding a prediction of the death of Jehoiakim and the certainty of Babylonian victory (Jer. 36:27-32).

Under Jehoiakim's evil rule the last hope for Judah ebbed away. The messages delivered during these years are full of darkest despair. God's heart is moved for His people, yet they *will not* respond.

Jer. 11:1–13:14. God's Covenant and oath given to Israel when His people came up from Egypt to freedom are reviewed, and the falseness of this generation to its oath is exposed. God will surely "uproot that nation, uproot and destroy it" (12:17).

Jer. 14:1–15:21. Much of the tone of despair in these messages is rooted in the growing realization that it is now too late for God's people to turn to

123

Him. God warns Jeremiah not even to pray for his countrymen and says, "Even though Moses and Samuel were to stand before Me, My heart would not be with this people; send them away from My presence and let them go!"

Four kinds of doom have been determined, and destiny has been sealed. They will go—

> Those destined for death, to death;
> And those destined for the sword, to the sword;
> And those destined for famine, to famine;
> And those destined for captivity, to captivity.
>
> *Jeremiah 15:1, 2*

Jer. 16:1–17:27. In view of the approaching judgment, Jeremiah is warned against taking a wife or having sons "in this place." In the Lord's goodness, his faithful servant will be spared the agony of seeing his own flesh and blood suffer in the coming invasion.

Jer. 22:1-30. Jeremiah visits the king to entreat him to practice justice, and when the king replies that he will not listen, Jeremiah pronounces judgment. No child of Jehoiakim will ever sit on the Davidic throne or rule in Jerusalem.

Jer. 23:1-40. The religious leaders whom God sent to care for His flock have instead scattered them. Their lying prophecies and promises will bring them everlasting reproach.

Jer. 25:1-38. Nebuchadnezzar is now identified as the invader about whom Jeremiah has been warning for some twenty-three years. Not only Judah, but also the surrounding nations, will suffer at his hand, for God has determined to use the Babylonians to punish the sins of Palestine.

Jer. 26:1-24. Jeremiah relates an incident from early in Jehoiakim's reign, when he had offered pardon if only the people would return to God and "listen to Me, to walk in My law, which I have set before you, to listen to the words of My servants the prophets whom I have been sending to you again and again" (26:4, 5).

The leaders then encouraged all the people to shout for Jeremiah's death for the "crime" of speaking against their city in God's name. The one man who dared to speak up in support of Jeremiah, Uriah, was himself hunted down and later killed by Jehoiakim. Yet Jeremiah was delivered, as God had promised at the time of his call.

Jer. 35:1-19. As an object lesson, Jeremiah gathers a family called the Rechabites, who had been commanded generations earlier by their clan leader not to drink wine. They had faithfully obeyed him.

Jeremiah pointed out the tragic difference: the Rechabites had faithfully obeyed a man, while Judah faithlessly disobeyed God Himself. For their faithfulness the Rechabites are promised God's constant favor. And Judah is promised judgment.

The nation has made its choice. Jeremiah will live to see the foretold results of his countrymen's sin. He will continue to raise his voice to guide them and show them the way of least pain. It may be that the severity of Judah's judgment will bring men to their senses and lead them to return to God.

GOING DEEPER

to personalize

1. Jeremiah's message must be read to sense its full impact. This week, concentrate on reading the text itself, guided by the charts on pages 119 and 123. Selecting from these charts, (a) read two of the four messages under Josiah, and (b) read five of the eleven messages under Jehoiakim.

2. Underline phrases and sections in these passages that seem particularly significant to you.

3. Select from your reading three verses or short passages which you would like to memorize for your own benefit. Memorize them.

to probe

1. Research the early days of the Babylonian Empire. What is its history, accomplishments, etc.?

2. Search out biographical material in the Book of Jeremiah and do a personality sketch of the prophet. What factors do you think might have been instrumental in shaping his personality? Write up your ideas in a five- to eight-page paper.

10

Jeremiah 21, 24, 27-29, 34, 37-44, 49-52
Ezekiel 1–24

EXILE

BY 597 B.C., IT WAS STUNNINGLY CLEAR that all
Jeremiah had prophesied for the past thirty years
was true. The most distinguished families in Judah
were taken to Babylon in the first of three deportations. Zedekiah, Judah's last king, was destined to
rule only eleven more years.

During these eleven years, Jeremiah continued to
warn God's people. He advised submission to
Babylonia, since God had chosen this pagan power
to discipline His people. But in spite of the evidence
of fulfilled prophecy, the Jews and their leaders
refused to listen. Zedekiah rebelled, and in 586 the
city fell. Zedekiah's children were executed while he
watched, and then he was blinded so that the last
thing he saw would be their deaths. Temple trea-
sures were transported to Babylon; both city and
Temple were razed. All but the poorest of the land
were taken into captivity, and Gedaliah was ap-
pointed as governor over the remnant. Again,

Jeremiah remained to guide them with God's Word.

In yet another uprising in 581 B.C., Gedaliah was killed along with the small Babylonian occupation force. Terrified at the revenge this act would surely bring, the remaining Jews fled toward Egypt. Jeremiah was forced to accompany them. Although they asked Jeremiah to seek God's guidance for them, they again rejected God's Word.

The portrait Jeremiah sketches of that incident is a fitting climax to the decades of Judah's denial of God. Looking back on it, we see the people "both great and small" respectfully approach the sixty-seven-year-old prophet. "Please let our petition come before you," they said, "and pray for us to the Lord your God, that is for all this remnant; because we are left but a few out of many, as your own eyes now see us, that the Lord your God may tell us the way in which we should walk and the thing that we should do" (42:1-3).

Jeremiah agreed to pray, and the people promised, "May the Lord be a true and faithful witness against us, if we do not act in accordance with the whole message with which the Lord your God will send you to us. Whether it is pleasant or unpleasant, we will listen to the voice of the Lord our God to whom we are sending you, in order that it may go well with us when we listen to the voice of the Lord our God" (42:5, 6).

But the message Jeremiah returned was not what the remnant expected. They were told not to fear the king of Babylon: God would keep them from punishment and restore them to their lands. They

JEREMIAH'S MESSAGES
DURING ZEDEKIAH'S REIGN

ch. 21	Advice for the king
ch. 24	Zedekiah abandoned
ch. 27	Judah must submit
ch. 28	God's iron yoke
ch. 29	Letter to the exiles
chs. 30—33	The new covenant
ch. 34	Judah's broken covenant
chs. 37—39	Jerusalem's fall
ch. 49	The nations warned

UNDER GEDELIAH

chs. 40—42	The flight to Egypt
chs. 43, 44	In Egypt

LATER

chs. 50, 51	The judgment of Babylon

were definitely *not* to flee to Egypt, for if they did, sword and famine would overtake them and they would die there with no survivors.

What was the reaction to this promise of protection? As soon as Jeremiah finished telling the people these words of the Lord, the leaders "and all the arrogant men" shouted at Jeremiah, "You are telling a lie! The Lord our God has not sent you to say, 'You are not to enter Egypt to reside there'; but Baruch the son of Neriah is inciting you against us to give us over into the hand of the Chaldeans, so they may put us to death or exile us to Babylon" (43:2, 3).

Rejecting God's Word, they plunged on into Egypt, dragging the prophet with them.

129

In Egypt, Jeremiah continued to minister, reminding the people of the sins of their fathers that had brought the judgment and warning against the punishment that must come to them in Egypt. Their response demonstrates the justice of God, who acts only when there is no hope of response or change in His people. Judah had gone too far in its commitment to sin.

> Then all the men who were aware that their wives were burning sacrifices to other gods, along with all the women who were standing by, as a large assembly, including all the people who were living in Pathros in the land of Egypt, responded to Jeremiah saying, "As for the message that you have spoken to us in the name of the Lord, we are not going to listen to you! But rather we will certainly carry out every word that has proceeded from our mouths, by burning sacrifices to the queen of heaven and pouring out libations to her, just as we ourselves, our forefathers, our kings and our princes did in the cities of Judah and in the streets of Jerusalem; for then we had plenty of food, and were well off, and saw no misfortune. But since we stopped burning sacrifices to the queen of heaven and pouring out libations to her, we have lacked everything and have met our end by the sword and by famine."
>
> *Jeremiah 44:15-18*

A saddened and angry Jeremiah then made a final statement.

"As for the smoking sacrifices that you burned in the cities of Judah and in the streets of Jerusalem, you and your forefathers, your kings and your princes, and the people of the land, did not the Lord remember them, and did not all this come into His mind? So the Lord was no longer able to endure it, because of the evil of your deeds, because of the abominations which you have committed; thus your land has become a ruin, an object of horror and a curse, without an inhabitant, as it is this day."

Jeremiah 44:21, 22

The final calamity now fell. Pharaoh Hophra, the Egyptian king who had welcomed Judah, was given over to his enemies, and sword and famine destroyed the Jewish colony that had committed themselves to perform their vows, not to the God who loved them, but to the pagan idols that had been their downfall.

And Jeremiah?

Tradition tells us that he found his way to Babylon and there completed his book, including his eyewitness story of the last days of Judah, recorded for the exiles—and for us.

THE FINAL DECADES
597 B.C.–581 B.C.

The messages recorded in the Book of Jeremiah during these decades show God's continuing concern for his people and their continuing rebelliousness. But there are also several new dimen-

131

sions. God's promises are reaffirmed (a feature we will explore in the next chapter) and His judgments on the pagan nations as well as Judah explained. Babylon itself, the scourge in God's hand, has gone beyond His purpose in ravaging Judah. Victory brought Babylon only pride: God's hand remained unrecognized and unrespected:

> Therefore behold, days are coming
> When I shall punish the idols of Babylon;
> And her whole land will be put to shame,
> And all her slain will fall in her midst.
>
> *Jeremiah 51:47*

EZEKIEL
Minister to the Exiles

At the time of the first deportation, twenty-five-year-old Ezekiel, a member of an important priestly family, was taken to Babylon along with those distinguished men whom Nebuchadnezzar wanted to remove from political influence in the homeland.

Some five years later, Ezekiel was called as a prophet (Ezek. 1:2). The year was 592 B.C.

Ezekiel had a unique two-part ministry. He prophesied a message of warning about Jerusalem's destruction between 592 and 586. His last message of this era, reported in Ezekiel 32, was delivered in April, 585 B.C., just after the city and its Temple fell.

For thirteen years Ezekiel was silent. Then in April of 572 B.C. the prophet took up a new ministry of hope, promise, and comfort for the exiles.

132

But it is on the first part that we need to focus now—ministry in which he struggled in Babylon, as his contemporary Jeremiah struggled in Judah, to lead God's people to accept captivity as His plan for them.

The Book of Ezekiel has four natural divisions.

Symbolic acts. One of the most striking features of Ezekiel are the symbolic acts that accompanied the prophet's messages.

Ezekiel did not simply speak of a coming siege of Jerusalem: he obtained a large brick, sketched the city on it, and like a child with a sandbox, raised earthen siege works against it. Lying on his side, he gazed at the besieged city, each day representing a year in God's program of discipline.

To represent the fate of the people still in Palestine, Ezekiel carefully shaved off his hair and beard. With greatest care he weighed and divided the hairs of his head. One-third of it he placed in the center of his sandbox city and burned: this represented those who would die when the Babylonians finally overran it. Another third, Ezekiel spread on the ground around the city and attacked it with a sword. Finally, Ezekiel took the last third and tossed it high to be scattered by the wind. This represented those who would be taken to surrounding nations and scattered across the face of the earth.

The exiles must have gathered in wonder to watch these strange actions of Ezekiel and then to listen as he, God's spokesman, explained their meaning. The message was clear: there would be no "next year in

OUTLINE OF EZEKIEL
I. Prophecies against Israel* (chs. 1—24)
II. Prophecies against foreign nations (chs. 25—32)
III. Prophecies of restoration (chs. 33—39)
IV. Prophecies of the messianic Temple (chs. 40—48)

MESSAGES TO THE CAPTIVES BEFORE 586

chs. 4, 5	Pictures of siege
chs. 6, 7	A desolate land
chs. 8—11	God withdraws from the Temple
ch. 12	Exile symbolized
ch. 13	False prophets charged
15:1—16:52	Jerusalem allegories
chs. 17—19	Leadership allegories
ch. 23	The two sisters
ch. 24	Death of Ezekiel's wife

* During the time of the surviving kingdom, *Israel* as well as *Judah* refers to the Jews left in the land, or to the whole Hebrew family.

Jerusalem" for those taken to Babylon.

The Temple vision (Ezek. 8-11). One of the most striking of the messages of this time is found in chapters 8—11. Ezekiel, sitting with the elders of the Jews in Babylon, was suddenly caught up by an angelic visitor and taken in a vision to Jerusalem. There he was shown what was happening in the very Temple in which the exiles had put their trust, confident that God would never permit the destruction of the building that had been His place of presence on earth.

The vision demonstrated how foolhardy such a hope was, for Ezekiel saw God removing His presence from the Temple. The remaining shell of marble and gold afforded no protection to God's

134

sinning people.

Ezek. 8:4-18. Ezekiel was taken to the Temple, where he perceived the glory of the Lord (the sign of His presence) in the Holy of Holies. But Ezekiel was told to look away from God and to observe what the men of Judah were doing in the Temple itself.

He was taken through a secret passage into a hidden chamber where the very elders of Israel worshiped idols and "creeping things and beasts and detestible things" (most likely the gods of Egypt that Jehovah had shown so powerless at the time of the Exodus). In the hidden chamber, the priests and elders offered incense, imagining that "the Lord does not see us; the Lord has forsaken the land."

Then Ezekiel was guided to the gate of the Temple, where he found women involved in the worship rites of the mother/son cult of Tammuz.

Then in the inner court he found twenty-five men facing *away* from the Temple (see 2 Chron. 6:20), praying toward the sun, the chief god Ra of the Egyptian pantheon.

The pollution of the Temple by the Hebrews showed how far all had fallen: "Therefore," God says, "I indeed shall deal in wrath. My eye will have no pity nor shall I spare" (Ezek. 8:18).

Ezek. 9:1-11. Then a striking thing happened. Six angelic figures with weapons in hand approached, and "the glory of the God of Israel went up from the cherub on which it had been, to the threshold of the Temple" (vs. 3). God's presence was about to leave!

The executioners were given instructions—first, to mark off those individuals who were ashamed and mourned over Judah's faithlessness, then to strike out among the rest and "utterly slay" those who had defiled the Lord's sanctuary.

Ezek. 10:1-22. Cherubim, a guard of honor, now approached the Temple, and the glory of the Lord moved out to the threshold. As the honor guard stood ready, the glory of the Lord left the Temple threshold and paused above it.

Ezek. 11:1-21. Ezekiel was now lifted and brought to the place from which the glory looked back toward the Temple. From this perspective, he saw the faces of the twenty-five who had earlier been worshiping the sun. Among them, he recognized the key religious and political leaders of God's people! Commanded to prophesy against them, Ezekiel spoke . . . and at his words one leader fell dead.

The prophet in turn cried out: "Alas, Lord God! Wilt Thou bring the remnant of Israel to a complete end?" (v. 13).

God's answer was both comforting and foreboding. Not all His people would be destroyed. Those in captivity would be kept secure and regathered one day to the Promised Land. But for those "whose hearts go after their detestable things and abominations," there would be a complete end.

Ezek. 11:22-25. With this announcement the cherubim lifted up their wings and the glory of the Lord left not only the Temple but the city itself, hesitating briefly over the mountains east of Jerusalem.

God had left His sinning people to the fate that, in their hardness of heart, they themselves had chosen.

GOING DEEPER

to personalize

1. Relive the last days in Judah with Jeremiah. From the chart on page 129, select four of the nine messages to read; also read chapters 40—44.

2. Imagine yourself to be Baruch, Jeremiah's secretary. Write a description of the prophet and his feelings and reactions as this intimate friend might have observed them.

3. Can you think of any ways in which you live under pressures similar to those known by Jeremiah? What are they?

4. Sample Ezekiel's writings as well. Read chapters 4, 5, 8—11 and select two additional passages from the remaining seven listed on page 134.

5. What picture do you develop of the exiles from Ezekiel's writings? Were they like or unlike the people left in Palestine?

to probe

1. Make a complete list of all the symbolic actions found in Ezekiel 1—24. Include the meaning of each, and how it communicated meaning to the exiles.

2. Ezekiel 8 describes worship of a number of false gods and goddesses associated with several pagan worship systems. Research to discover what each described action indicates about the religious practices and beliefs of the people of Judah at this time.

SPRINGTIME COMING

WITH THE DESTRUCTION OF THE TEMPLE and the final flight of the few who remained in Palestine, all hope for Israel seemed dead.

But now each of the two great prophets who spoke to this people shared a message of hope! That generation was experiencing punishment for sin. But a new generation would arise. And, in a time to come, God's people would return to His Promised Land. There they would know the fullness of the blessing God had yearned to pour out on the exiles. The men and women of Jeremiah and Ezekiel's time had placed their trust in the Temple; now they were called to put their trust in the God of the ancient covenants.

THE COVENANTS

As many people in our own day, the Hebrews seem to have lost their identity when they experienced prosperity. Now the ministry of the prophets had to do with the recovery of that identity: the rediscovery of the fact that they must understand themselves and act as God's covenant people.

The Abrahamic Covenant. God called Abraham out of Ur of the Chaldees and led him into Palestine. There an original promise given to Abraham was reaffirmed and expanded. Looking at these early Genesis promises to Abraham and his descendants, we see several critical features:

- Abraham is to be progenitor of a great nation.
- Abraham is to be blessed and his name made great.
- Abraham is to be the source of blessing for the world.
- Abraham's treatment by others is to be the criterion for their own blessing or curse.
- Abraham's descendants are to possess the land of Palestine.
- Abraham's descendants are to have a special relationship with God "throughout their generations."

These promise elements, found in Genesis 12, 15, and 17, are the core of the Hebrew identity. They are the solid rock on which the entire Old Testament is founded. All the Old Testament writers and prophets share a common conviction that God is working out His plan in our world and that His plan is revealed in the covenant promises given to Abraham and his descendants.

The confidence of the Jew in Jeremiah's day should never have been in the fact that God's Temple was in their land—as though God set a greater store by gilded marble than by His oath. Instead, the Hebrew confidence and sense of identity needed to be rooted in God Himself and His trustworthiness. Surely God would fulfill His promised purpose; surely meaning in life might be found in commitment to *being* a covenant people.

The Davidic Covenant. The promises given to Abraham revealed the purpose that God had eternally in mind. As the decades and centuries passed, additional insights into God's plan were given. In the time of King David, for instance, another dimension of God's plan was revealed. A deliverer for Israel and for mankind would be born of David's line. This deliverer would one day assume the throne of his father and reign as king over Israel and the entire world. In his days, there would be peace—peace that would never be broken.

After the days of David, fresh insights concerning this king were added by the prophets. Micah and others told God's people that the king would actually be their God: that from Bethlehem, the city of David, "One will go forth for Me to be ruler in Israel. His goings forth are from long ago, from the days of eternity." This One would come to "shepherd His flock in the strength of the Lord, in the majesty of the name of the Lord His God." It is this One who "will be our peace" (Mic. 5:1-5).

And so the purpose of God, a purpose that will one day be realized, had been explained to God's people. Through their stock, the Messiah, God's Anointed One, would come to deliver all mankind from sin and suffering. All history marched toward that culminating end.

But now, joltingly, the people of God had been removed from the Promised Land. How could God fulfill His promises? David's family lived no longer in Bethlehem. There was no throne for a royal descendant to mount. The very existence of the nation God had promised Abraham had ceased, and the conqueror, rather than suffer divine judgment, seemed only to prosper.

The believing Jew, who had anchored his faith in God and found his identity in the ancient covenants, as well as the ungodly Jew, who had mistaken ritual for reality, was stunned by the exile. Had God cast off His people? Had the very covenants themselves been set aside because of the abominations of their nation?

The Mosaic Covenant. Part of the answer to these soul-searching questions of the exiles is found in understanding the nature of the Covenant of Law.

Both the Abrahamic and Davidic Covenants were in fact promises—promises that God would fulfill the purposes each expressed. As such, neither of these hinged on man's actions. Whatever the response of the Chosen People, God had preannounced His plan, and he would accomplish it.

The Mosaic Covenant is not like this at all. It is not an unconditional promise; it does not focus on the culmination of history or the purposes God has settled on for the end of time. Instead, the

141

Mosaic Covenant is an existential covenant: it speaks to each living generation afresh, and it is designed to guide each generation to *experience the blessings of the end-time in their "now."* By responding to God as He spoke the laws and statues that showed Israel how to live in love and justice, the people of Israel would be in the place of blessing. By rejecting those laws and statues, by adopting a life-style of indifference and injustice, a given generation would find itself approaching judgment. God would pour out on the obedient generation all the good things destined for mankind at history's end; He would pour out on the disobedient generation all the misery that sin deserves.

RELATIONSHIP BETWEEN THE COVENANTS

Other Covenants	*Law Covenant*
1. God only maker	1. Each generation/ individual enters it with Him
2. Future in view	2. Present experience in view
3. Unconditional promise	3. Conditional, with promises and warnings

By understanding the relationship between the covenants of promise and the Mosaic Covenant of law, the Hebrew people (and we) can understand the vital truth that both Jeremiah and Ezekiel take pains to emphasize. The exile was a punishment and discipline brought on by generations of disobedience. However long its sufferings might continue, *the exile in no way changed the purposes or the promises of God.* The people had been torn from the land? Then their children would go back!

They had through disobedience forfeited their own part of the promised blessing given by God through Moses. Yet in some future generation God would bring to pass all that He had promised to Abraham and David. Rather than casting doubt on the future of Israel, the exile should have reassured. It demonstrated conclusively that *God does keep His Word.*

How these words from the ancient Book of Deuteronomy must have echoed through the minds of the people of the exile:

The Lord will bring you and your king whom you shall set over you to a nation which neither you or your fathers have known, and there you shall serve other gods, wood and stone. And you shall become a horror, a proverb, and a taunt among all the people where the Lord will drive you. . . .

. . . Because you did not serve the Lord your God with joy and a glad heart, for the abundance of all things; therefore you shall serve your enemies whom the Lord shall send against you, in hunger, in thirst, in nakedness, and in the lack of all things; and He will put an iron yoke on your neck until He has destroyed you.

The Lord will bring a nation against you from afar, from the end of the earth, as the eagle swoops down, a nation whose language you shall not understand, a nation of fierce countenance who shall have no respect for the old, nor show favor to the young . . . .

. . . Moreover, the Lord will scatter you among all peoples, from one end of the earth to the other end of the earth; and there you shall serve other gods, wood and stone, which you or your fathers have not known. And among those nations you shall find no rest, and there shall be no resting place for the sole of your foot; but there the Lord will give you a trembling heart, failing of eyes, and despair of soul. So your life shall hang in doubt before you; and you shall be in dread night and day, and shall have no assurance of your life. In the morning you shall say, "Would that it were evening!" And at evening you shall say, "Would that it were morning!" because of the dread of your heart.

Deuteronomy 28:36, 37, 47-50, 64-67

Yet words from the same book brought comfort:

So it shall become when all of these things have come upon you, the blessing and the curse which I have set before you, and you call them to mind in all nations where the Lord your God has banished you, and you return to the Lord your God and obey Him with all your heart and soul according to all that I command you today, you and your sons, then the Lord your God will restore you from captivity, and have compassion on you, and

will gather you again from all the peoples where
the Lord your God has scattered you. If your
outcasts are at the ends of the earth, from there
the Lord your God will gather you, and from
there He will bring you back.

Deuteronomy 30:1-4

The unchanging purposes of God will be fulfilled
and his covenants kept. A generation might die in
exile. But the Israel would be preserved.

THE NEW COVENANT
Jeremiah 30–33

Now God chose Jeremiah, the prophet of doom,
to bring to Israel yet another expansion of the
Abrahamic Covenant. At a time when His people
were torn from the land, as foretold a thousand
years earlier by Moses, God gave them through
Jeremiah additional and fresh revelation about the
fulfillment of His promise.

The timing was significant. There could be no
doubt that God had *not* cast off Israel forever. The
content of the new revelation was significant also.
Earlier, God had explained that fulfillment of His
plan involved a messianic king. Now God explained
that fulfillment of His plan involved replacing the
whole Mosaic system with a New Covenant that
would plant righteousness within the personality of
the believer.

Jer. 30:1-11. God promised that His people Israel
would be brought "back to the land that I gave to

145

their forefathers, and they shall possess it." In that final regathering, "David their king, whom I will raise up for them" would lead them to serve the Lord. In the exile God would "chasten you justly," but will "not destroy you completely."

Jer. 30:12-24. The wound of God's people was incurable and their iniquity great. As a result, the captivity was absolutely necessary. But again, the promise was given that Israel would return, "and you shall be My people, and I will be your God."

Yet God's wrath had to be experienced until His purpose of purification was accomplished: "in the latter days you will understand this" (v. 24).

Jer. 31:1-14. The blessings of the time of regathering are described, and the promise made that the full extent of the Promised Land will be theirs.

Jer. 31:28-34. Here is the heart of the New Covenant, which is shown in the Book of Hebrews to have been confirmed by the blood of Christ.

> "The time is coming, says the Lord,
>   when I will make a new covenant
> with the house of Israel
>   and with the house of Judah.
> It will not be like the covenant I made with their
>   forefathers
>   when I took them by the hand to lead them
>   out of Egypt,
> because they did not remain faithful to my cov-
>   enant,
>   and I turned away from them,
>   says the Lord.

This is the covenant I will make with the house
of Israel
after that time, says the Lord.
I will put my laws in their minds
and write them on their hearts.
I will be their God,
and they will be my people.
No longer will a man teach his neighbor,
or a man his brother, saying, 'Know the
Lord,'
because they will all know me,
from the least of them to the greatest.
I will forgive their wickedness,
and will remember their sins no more."

Hebrews 8:8-12

With this great promise, yet another dimension of the Abrahamic Covenant is unfolded: the time is coming when all will be "born again" and a new heart given. Only then, when "the least of them to the greatest of them" shall know the Lord, will God's good purposes for mankind by fulfilled.

Jer. 32:1-44. With the city of Jerusalem under siege, Jeremiah purchased a field and buried the deed in an earthen pot so that it will "last a long time" (v. 14).

This action demonstrated to the people of Jerusalem that even though the city would fall and the people be carried into exile, "houses and fields and vineyards shall again be bought in this land" (v. 15).

Jeremiah's prayer (vs. 16-25) is a highlight of this

147

chapter, as is God's response: "Behold, I will gather them in My anger, and My wrath, and in great indignation; and I will bring them back to this place and make them dwell in safety. And they shall be My people, and I will be their God; and I will give them one heart and one way, that they may fear Me always, for their own good, and for the good of their children after them. And I will make an everlasting covenant with them that I will not turn away from them—to do them good; and I will put the fear of Me in their hearts so that they will not turn away from Me" (vs. 37-40).

Jer. 33:1-13. Again comes the promise of restoration. "I will restore the fortunes of Judah and the fortunes of Israel. . . . And I will cleanse them from all their iniquity by which they have sinned against Me, and I will pardon all their iniquities" (vs. 7, 8).

Jer. 33:14-22. The Davidic Covenant is reaffirmed, and David is promised never to "lack a man to sit on the throne" (v. 17). This promise is not that a descendant of David will always rule in Jerusalem, but that there will always be a valid claimant—until finally, in fulfillment of all the covenant promises, Messiah reigns.

Jer. 33:23-26. With the reaffirmation of the Davidic Covenant comes also reaffirmation of God's intention to accomplish His purposes through the physical seed of Abraham—the peoples of Israel and Judah. The fulfillment of God's promises to the descendants of Abraham, Isaac, and Jacob are just as certain as the fact that night follows day. "I will restore their fortunes and will have mercy" (v. 26).

148

And so through Jeremiah, the man who announced the exile, came the great promise of regathering and the promise of a New Covenant, in
which the laws once written in stone would be rewrit-
ten on the very hearts of men born again into living
relationship with God.

SHALL THESE BONES LIVE?
Ezekiel 33–48

Some thirteen years after the destruction of
Jerusalem and the Temple, Ezekiel took up a new
ministry. Before, he had warned the exiles to accept
the fact that they would live, and die, in captivity.
Now his message was one of hope. The captivity was
not permanent; a remnant would return to the land.
In His own time, God would fulfill the promise
given to Abraham and David.

Restoration promised (Ezek. 33–39). A series of messages look into the future to show a revised Israel.
Two are particularly significant.

Ezek. 37:1-14. Ezekiel is taken by the Spirit to a
valley. Scattered over it are millions of bones, dried
and lifeless on the ground. Commanded by God,
Ezekiel cries out for the bones to hear the Word of
the Lord. In response comes a great rattling as the
bones come together. Then sinews grow, and flesh
and skin to cover them. Finally, the winds breathe
life into the restored beings, and they "stood on their
feet, an exceedingly great army" (v. 10).

God explains the vision: "These bones are the
whole house of Israel; behold, they say, 'Our bones

149

are dried up, and our hope has perished. We are completely cut off' " (v. 11). Ezekiel is to inform them that God will open the graves (the lands to which they have been scattered) and bring them back to the land of Israel. The restored Israel will at first be lifeless. Then God will act again. "And I will put My Spirit within you, and you will come to life, and I will place you on your own land" (v. 14). However hopeless the situation seems, God is able to make the dead bones live.

Ezek. 38, 39. Ezekiel sees not only the return of the exiles; he sees beyond to yet another time of testing, when armies will again march against Palestine and only God's intervention will deliver. The promise of return and blessing is *not* to be viewed by the exiles as an immediate fulfillment of the covenant promises. History will stretch out for further centuries, even millenniums. But each scattering of Israel will be followed by a regathering. And so Ezekiel gives God's final promise:

"When I bring them back from the peoples and gather them from the land of their enemies, then I shall be sanctified through them in the sight of the many nations. Then they will know that I am the Lord their God because I made them go into exile among the nations, and then gathered them again to their own land; and I will leave none of them there any longer. And I will not hide My face from them any longer, for I shall have poured out My Spirit on the house of Israel."

Ezek. 39:27-29

The millennial temple (Ezek. 40–48). These nine chapters make up one of the most controversial sections of Scripture. It looks forward to the time of the end and describes a temple in Jerusalem on a renewed and restored earth. The description constantly intermingles natural and supernatural, describing a world very unlike the one we now know—a world in which "the Lord is there" (48: 35).

Much of the controversy surrounds the sacrificial system—which in the end-time would be unnecessary, because Christ's one sacrifice in making the New Covenant was sufficient to perfect all who believe in Him (Heb. 10). The best way to look at the sacrifices and ceremonies of Ezekiel 42—46 seems to be as memorials, a constant and joyous reminder of a redemption that has been secured. Seen in this context, Ezekiel's picture of the final kingdom is parallel to the vision of Isaiah 60 and an affirmation of a theme seen much in both Jeremiah and Ezekiel. The final glorious kingdom can be realized only through God's personal presence among the redeemed, when the "tabernacle of God is with men" (Rev. 21: 3, KJV).

How rich life will be when Jesus comes, and the full meaning of Ezekiel's promise is experienced by all: "I will not hide my face any more from them any longer, for I shall have poured out My Spirit on the house of Israel" (39: 29).

GOING DEEPER
to personalize
1. Review Deuteronomy 28—30. What aspects of

151

these chapters would have been particularly meaningful to the exiles?

2. Study carefully the key chapters of Jeremiah 30—33. What indications can you find in these chapters that the elements of the Abrahamic and Davidic Covenants pointed out on pages 139-41 are still in force? From your study, how would you evaluate the following position: "God has set aside the Jews, and now Christians have been given the covenant blessings in spiritual rather than physical form"?

3. Many believe that the pattern of dispersion and regathering does not refer simply to the Babylonian exile but in fact illustrates God's way of dealing with His Old Testament people at all times. According to this theory, the Jews have undergone a similar scattering since the first century A.D. and only now are seeing a regathering in which the bones are taking on flesh in modern Israel—but do not yet have spiritual life.

Two of the passages used to support this idea are the Deuteronomy passage and Ezekiel 38, 39. Study these passages, and see what you can find to support or refute it.

to probe

1. Hebrews 8: 1—10: 22 is a great New Testament passage that indicates that believers today do experience the benefits of the promised New Covenant through faith in Christ, just as Old Testament believers experienced the benefits of the Abrahamic Covenant when they obeyed the Law. Read this extended passage carefully, and write out what the

New Covenant means for you today.

2. Study Ezekiel 40—48. Read the text several times, and jot down your impressions and questions. Try to answer your own questions first; then look up discussions of these chapters in several commentaries. Take thoughtful notes.

Do not write a paper to hand in, but do hand in the notes you took as you read the passage, your thoughts about answers to your questions, and the notes you took from the commentaries.

THE VEIL OF TEARS

WHEN JEREMIAH FINALLY MADE HIS WAY to Babylon, he found the Hebrew people in far better condition than most of us might imagine. There were no concentration camps. There was no slave labor, as there had been in Egypt. Instead, the exiles were settled in southern Mesopotamia near the river Chebar, just southeast of Babylon. They enjoyed royal protection and a great amount of self-government. They married, kept in touch with Jerusalem (Jer. 29: 6), met to worship and discuss and kept the Sabbath. A. C. Schurltz describes their lives:

> Some of the captives were used to supply labor for Nebuchadnezzar's many building projects, at least in the beginning of the exile. Some of them enjoyed special prerogatives. They could own their homes and land, and enjoy the produce of their gardens (Jer. 29: 4, 7; Ezek. 8: 1; 12: 1-7). This would enable them to provide for some of their physical needs. Some of the captives apparently made an adequate living in other

ways (Zech. 6:9-11), and even entered business in the "city of merchants," as Babylon was known (Ezek. 17:4, 12). The Hebrew banking house of Murashu appears in the inscriptions. The lists of captives receiving royal support includes along with the Hebrew names the skilled trades in which some of them worked. Jeremiah 29:5-7 indicates that they were so successful financially that they were able to send money to Jerusalem, and when the exiles were given permission by Cyrus to return home, they refused because according to Josephus "they were not willing to leave their possessions" (Jos. Antiq. XI.i.3). This materialism on the part of some of the exiles led to conformity to the customs of the Babylonians and cultural assimilation. The tendency to assimilate included the adoption of the Aramaic language and the acceptance of idolatry and participation in pagan ceremonies, even to sacrificing their sons on pagan altars (Ezek. 14:3-5; 20:31).[1]

Yet the experience was for many of the exiles an increasingly bitter one. After the destruction of Jerusalem and its Temple, when all hope of return seemed gone, the people of Israel began to realize how much they had lost. The birthright they had so lightly traded away for pagan Baals and Asherahs suddenly seemed precious. Israel realized at last that if they were not God's people, they had no identity. If they no longer retained the promises, life had no meaning.

This sense of loss is communicated in the brief Book of Lamentations, which tradition tells us was written by Jeremiah himself.

1. *Zondervan Pictorial Bible Encyclopedia*, vol. 2, p. 427.

How lonely sits the city
That was full of people!
She has become like a widow
Who once was great among the nations!
She who was a princess among the provinces
Has become a forced laborer!
She weeps bitterly in the night,
And her tears are on her cheeks;
She has none to comfort her
Among all her lovers.
All her friends have dealt treacherously with
    her,
They have become her enemies.
Judah has gone into exile under affliction,
And under harsh servitude;
She dwells among the nations,
But she has found no rest;
All her pursuers have overtaken her
In the midst of distress.
. . . .
Her adversaries have become her masters,
Her enemies prosper;
For the Lord has caused her grief
Because of the multitude of her transgressions;
Her little ones have gone away
As captives before the adversary,
And all her majesty
Has departed from the daughter of Zion.

Lamentations 1:1-3, 5, 6

Looking at the change, the captives finally appreciated the life-style that God had planned for them under His own care. Lamenting, the people sorrowed now for what they had once scorned.

> The law is no more;
> Also, her prophets find
> No vision from the Lord.
> The elders of the daughter of Zion
> Sit on the ground, they are silent.
> They have thrown dust on their heads;
> They have girded themselves with sackcloth.
> The virgins of Jerusalem
> Have bowed their heads to the ground.
> My eyes fail because of tears.
> My spirit is greatly troubled;
> My heart is poured out on the earth,
> Because of the destruction of the daughter of
>   my people.
>
> *Lamentations 2:9-11*

Suddenly the material things that had tempted Judah seemed meaningless. In setting their hearts on wealth, they had seemed for a time to gain the whole world. But they had lost themselves.

IMPACT OF THE EXILE

The tears shed by Israel in Babylon proved fruitful. Israel's repentance brought many benefits to God's people and in significant ways shaped the nation up to and even beyond the days of Christ.

A remnant. As Josephus pointed out, many of the materialistic Jews found Babylon a trade center in which they prospered. These wealthy men and women settled down to enjoy their new life-style, untroubled by questions about the ultimate meaning of their lives. When the time came for God's promise of a return to be fulfilled, only those who were moved by a deep religious commitment were ready to go. These returned, eager to lay the foundations of a new Temple and to rebuild Jerusalem, sensing that only when God's people were again in the Promised Land could Messiah come.

Thus the decades in Babylon, like the destruction of the wicked in Jerusalem some seventy years earlier, served to cleanse and purify the nation.

That the purification process was accomplished is demonstrated by the fact that, in spite of tremendous pressures later, the Jewish people successfully resisted every effort to make them give up their Law and accept Hellenistic culture.

The tendency to chase after the gods of the peoples around them was thoroughly purged by the Exile.

The written Law. Prior to the Captivity, the Levites had been charged with the responsibility of teaching the Law to the people. This function was shared with the priests, who were responsible for the Law's official interpretation.

But the religious life of the people had centered around the festivals and the Temple and its sacrifices. With the Temple destroyed and no place where sacrifices could be offered, the emphasis of the exiles shifted to the study and interpretation of the Law and the prophets. God's Word, which they had not listened to, was now studied intently and devoutly.

An example of this revival of biblical studies is seen in Ezra, who "set his heart to study the law of the Lord, and to practice it, and to teach His statutes and ordinances in Israel" (Ezra 7:10). Later scribes would amass volumes of traditions supposedly containing an "oral law" given to Moses at Sinai, which would rob the written Law of its meaning. But during the Captivity and in the years immediately following, the hearts of many in Israel were set to study, to do, and to teach God's book. Clearly, all that had happened to the people of Israel and Judah had happend in accordance with what had been written. Clearly, too, if one wished to live in harmony with God and experience blessing rather than judgment, the words of God must be taken to heart.

This fervor for the Law, even though later twisted and misguided, was one of the positive outcomes of the Exile.

The synagogue system. While there is no definite evidence of the existence of the synagogue as an institution prior to the Hellenistic age, it seems most likely that its origins go back to the time of Babylonian Captivity.

With the Temple gone, groups of faithful people met in homes in their exile, and when Israel returned to their homeland, this new institution seems to have been retained. Many modern excavations indicate that before the Christian era the synagogue was the center of town life. Here the sacred books were read and often interpreted by a rabbi. Here the

159

townsmen gathered to work out legal-political problems, guided by the books of revelation. In fact, on the return from Babylon by Persian royal decree, the Law of Moses was made civilly binding on the Jews living west of the Euphrates.

By Jesus' day, each town was also responsible for seeing that the children learned to read the sacred Word, so that on becoming an adult, each male might take on responsibility for himself and the community.

The synagogue system has continued to our own day. This institution, springing from the exile, maintains a continuing impact on Judaism.

In each of these ways, then, the Captivity proved of lasting benefit to God's people. It purged Israel of her tendency to idolatry. It refocused Israel's attention on the Word of God. It shaped institutions that in the future would hold the Jewish people together when a much greater and longer exile should come. God's punishments, like His blessings, are designed to bring good to His beloved people.

DEMONSTRATION OF PRINCIPLE

As suggested in the last chapter, it is also helpful to look at Israel's experience in Babylon as a demonstration of a basic principle of God's dealing with His Old Testament people.

The Deuteronomy warnings (chs. 28, 29) made it clear that responsiveness to God's Law was the condition of blessing for a given generation. The promises contained in the covenants would one day be fulfilled, but in the meantime, blessing for each generation was mediated through obedience to the Law. That same passage made it clear that a physical relationship to Abraham was not enough in itself to guarantee blessing. Each link in the line of descent must exercise an obedience-producing faith in God. And whatever might happen to a given generation, it would in no way change God's commitment to the purposes announced in His Word.

In Jeremiah's time, the Jews were led into captivity, torn from the Promised Land. *But God's promised purposes were unaffected.* Much later, just after the time of Christ, a Roman invader would destroy Jerusalem and another Temple. As a result, the Jewish people would again be scattered through the nations. There, "among those nations you shall find no rest, and there shall be no resting place for the sole of your foot; but there the Lord will give you a trembling heart, failing of eyes, and despair of soul" (Deut. 28:65). The words of Deuteronomy have echoed through our centuries, describing in mournful tone the experience of the Jewish people in the last nineteen hundred years. In Spain, in Poland, in Russia, in Nazi Germany—in whatever land—God's ancient people have found no rest. Only in our day, with the return to Palestine and the establishment in 1948 of the Jewish state, have we heard the dry bones rattle and watched the flesh and sinews and skin take shape.

The announcements of Jeremiah and Ezekiel, restating in a time of exile the promises on which Israel was founded, give us a new assurance that God will do for His people in our day *all* that His Word reveals to be their destiny.

It seems clear that the messages of the prophets who spoke before and during the first exile provided a unique reassurance to Israel—a reassurance we need to keep in mind when we study our Old Testament and our New. *God is faithful.* The purposes He has preannounced are in fact promises—promises God will keep. In keeping them, the future course of history will ever move toward its determined end. Neither detours into sin by God's chosen or the iniquities of the unbelieving can tilt the ages off their course.

God is faithful.

And God's will will be done.

GOING DEEPER

to personalize

1. The experience of Israel in exile demonstrates that even God's disciplinary actions are designed for our good. Can you think of a time God disciplined you—and good resulted? Jot down notes on the situation and its results.

2. How do you think a firm grasp of the fact that God is *faithful* might affect most believers today? What might its impact have been on Judah before the Exile? During the Exile?

3. What is the main impact on your own life of the realization that God is faithful?

4. Review quickly all the major messages of the prophets of the kingdom days. Make a listing of

these messages and beside each jot down one or more ways in which the message is applicable today. Use this kind of chart:

PROPHETIC MESSAGES

Prophet	Major Message	Meaning for Us Today

to probe

1. Check several reference works to find out all you can about the Exile and its results. In addition to listings under *Exile* and *Babylon*, check references to the synagogue, scribes, rabbis, oral law, etc.

2. Imagine yourself to be a citizen of Israel today. What might the prophecies we have explored in the last three chapters (in Jeremiah and Ezekiel) say to you? Write a five- to-eight-page paper explaining their modern impact.

THE LIVING WORD

IN THIS BOOK WE HAVE PURPOSELY AVOIDED a study of the prophets' picture of the future. It is true that the broad outline of future events sketched in the covenants is filled in to a great extent by the prophets. Yet, if we read the prophets simply to see what is ahead, we miss what most surely was their basic ministry. We miss the meaning of the message of each prophet to his own generation.

And so in this book (unlike *Springtime Coming,* the next book in this series), we have focused on the message of the prophets to their contemporaries and the deep concern God has with the life of His people in *this* world.

We need to review the central message briefly to make sure that the impact of the prophets for our own day has not been missed. These spokesmen for God communicated a *living* Word: a Word not only with meaning for people of the past but one that speaks in vital tones to you and me as well.

Here is a review of some of the messages and a highlighting of others we merely touched on.

GOD'S FAITHFULNESS

This theme was explored in the last chapter. Everything that happened to Israel happened in harmony with God's preannounced plan and purposes. The prophets were essentially interpreters who under God's guidance expanded and explained what God had already revealed. The fulfillment of their prophecies reinforced for Israel the portrait of a God who keeps His word.

In a very real way, the deep conviction that God is a covenant-keeping person is the major message of the prophets to us. There may be many aspects of God's plan that we do not yet fully understand. Like Israel, we may be tempted to lose hope when events seem to cast our generation adrift. Yet we have no way to measure the expanse of history's future— those generations (or months and years) God has set aside to complete His work. What we do have as an anchor for our own souls in time of stress is the conviction that God is faithful.

Jeremiah wept over the defeat of God's people and their exile from the land. Yet on God's command he purchased a field and buried the deed where it would be secure. Before another general could return to the Promised Land, Jeremiah would be in his grave. But there was no doubt in his mind that they would return. The covenant of God would be kept; the promises to His people would stand.

Today, you and I are recipients of promises as well. They are not the same promises; we are not Israel. But all that God tells us in His Word is completely trustworthy. God is a faithful person; He does not lie.

In some ways, our individual experience may duplicate the experiences of the nation Israel. There are times when we waver between wandering and revival. There are times when God disciplines. But God remains faithful to us, even as He was faithful to the Old Testament nation. He may send us away, but He will restore. And then we'll discover that even our times of exile were designed for our good.

If you and I have come into personal relationship with God through Jesus Christ, the maker of the New Covenant, then we can count on it. He will remain faithful.

We are His, and He will accomplish His purpose in our lives.

CONCERN FOR JUSTICE

One of the repeated themes emphasized by the prophets is God's commitment to justice and His desire for us to share this concern.

Too often evangelical Christians have made a distinction between what they see as God's concern for "souls" and for social issues. The argument has been based on several (valid) assumptions.

The first assumption is that the basic issue each individual must resolve is that of relationship with

God. Will a person come through faith to trust in God and receive the forgiveness salvation provides? Until that issue is resolved, all else is seen as relatively irrelevant. Because the eternal issue is the one that counts, the conditions of this life seem unimportant.

A second assumption is that focus on social conditions, even those which are admittedly unjust, may steal attention from the eternal. In the past, some Christians have become social activists to the extent that concern for man's relationship with God has been lost. Thus, many conservative Christians fear that social consciousness may lead to a new modernism in which the primary of the eternal is surrendered to fleeting, ever-changing social conditions—which, when resolved, always seem replaced by problems just as great.

A third assumption is that the only viable solution to social injustice is the transformation of individuals through personal relationship with God. In fact, the argument goes, injustice and oppression are the natural expression in society of the root problem of mankind: sin. And God deals with sin individually, giving men and women His life, transforming their motives, values, and character, and, as a result, their behavior. Thus, for many Christians an aggressive ministry of evangelism *is* an expression of concern for justice, concern which, if the evangelism is successful, will in time change the character of community and society.

There certainly is reason to appreciate the motives and honest intent with which such arguments

167

are offered and to recognize their elements of truth. Certainly there should be an overriding concern that individuals come into personal relationship with God. Man's eternal destiny hinges on this relationship; coming to trust Christ and to enter into New Covenant relationship does have priority. The biblical faith teaches us that long after this universe is dissolved, each human being will continue conscious existence. Certainly "Where will you spend eternity?" *is* more important than "Are you currently being oppressed?" It is also true that the just society does await the return of Christ to rule over a renewed humanity—one that has God's law written on its heart. No reform movement can bring Camelot—not the New Deal, the New Frontier, the Great Society, or any other dreams of men who seek to change through the environment what can be corrected only by a change within the human heart.

But to admit the validity of some of these arguments does not mean that the conclusions drawn from them are acceptable. In fact, the conclusions are *wrong,* and our lack of concern for justice represents a tragic failure to understand the character of God and the calling of the believer.

Several factors are generally ignored by Christians who attempt to justify lack of concern for justice:

1. A believer's concern for justice is not associated with utopian political or social theory. The Christian does not seek to "do justice" because he expects to bring in the Kingdom of God. Long after Judah and Israel had demonstrated that they had lost all con-

cern for persons and adopted selfish and materialistic values, Micah cried out to individuals,

> He has told you, O man, what is good;
> And what does the Lord require of you
> But to do justice, to love kindness,
> And walk humbly with your God?
>
> *Micah 6:8*

When, in England, Wilberforce initiated his long campaign to outlaw slavery in the empire, he did not do it as a social reformer. He was moved by Christian compassion; he acted because he *cared* about those helpless chattels that the majority in his day viewed as scarcely human. In working for justice, in showing lovingkindness, in committing his health and fortune to the betterment of his oppressed fellow man, this man uniquely pleased and honored God.

Not the utopian dream but *concern for people* drives us to justice.

2. It is tragically wrong to view the Christian's concern for justice as something to be valued or devalued on the basis of its contribution to evangelism. The church has often done this. We have said, "Send doctors—that we might break the power of the witch doctor and win the lost."

These statements implicitly assign to justice a value based on the *end* it is supposed to achieve. Thus "doing justice" is viewed as a means to an end, and when it does not seem to promote that end (evangelism), it is roughly thrust aside.

But is concern for the oppressed and the hungry a

169

tool by which we manipulate people? Do we really want to reach out to meet human needs or else to withhold help coldly and calculatingly?

How do we differ from the Pharisees if our commitment to do right by all men is conditional on whether we believe our actions will help us gain other ends? We do not "do justice" because it is a means to an end. We do justice because it is right.

3. It is an amazing thing that concern for people's social and material needs are conceived as somehow intrinsically different from concern for their souls. Part of the cause is a peculiar dichotomization that is not biblical. The Bible truly does not describe man as composed of some immaterial "soul" that is captured in a physical body and trapped into feeling emotions, hungers, drives, and motives. There is no division between the body and the "real person."

Instead, when the breath of life was breathed into the body God had prepared, "man became a living soul" (Gen. 2:7, KJV). Our eternal destiny is not "that we would be unclothed, but clothed upon" (2 Cor. 5:4, KJV), fully integrated with a resurrection body, emotions, will—all that makes us persons, shaped to bear God's image.

Our theology ought to teach us that we need to approach others as *persons*, not *souls*, and to realize that all we are and experience has impact on how we perceive God and relationship with Him. Strangely, an evangelism that comes to people with a verbal gospel of God's love but does not demonstrate that love in ways that can be experienced does not adequately represent God.

The point is simple. When we come in contact with others, we are to reach out to them in love and love them fully. We will care about their *every* need. It may be there is little we can do to change basic conditions in society. Reforming society may well be impossible. But we do not hold back in our loving of people because one sort of need is "social" and another "spiritual." If minority children in our neighborhood need tutoring, we do not ignore that need because such a ministry in our church would not be a "religious" program. If an inner-city store gouges poor people who cannot shop elsewhere, we do not keep silent because this injustice allegedly isn't related to their souls. If pornography is openly carried in a store near a high school, we do not ignore it.

The Christian has a commitment to justice because justice is right.

Strikingly, when we express an honest concern for the needs of others around us and show a personal willingness to become involved for their sakes, we also demonstrate in a compelling way the love of God. The enfleshed love of God, reaching out to care, *is* a vital and real part of the gospel.

4. Probably the most compelling reason the Christian today needs to be committed to doing right by others is this: that's the kind of person God is. God Himself is just. He is committed to doing right by all. God, as the Old Testament clearly reveals, does care deeply when injustice and indifference to others are accepted elements of an individual's or a society's life-style.

171

Sometimes this emphasis is set aside with the comment, "Oh, that's an Old Testament idea. You don't see it emphasized in the New." What an irrelevant and foolish remark! Has God changed? Does He no longer care? Is the God of the New Testament a different person than the God of the Old?

The whole biblical concept of justice, that God is committed to do right by all men, is rooted in the revelation that *God is just.* His essential character is involved. The New Testament does add new revelation and gives a far broader picture of God's eternal plan than did the Old. But the New and Old Testaments are never in conflict: instead, the New Testament *adds* facets of God's intentions without denying the Old. Thus, there is no way we might even *suggest* that anger at oppression and injustice, that judgment on a materialism that values things and uses persons, or that concern with the plight of our fellow man is no longer godly. "Pure and undefiled religion is the sight of our God and Father" is still "to visit orphans and widows in their distress, and to keep oneself unstained by the world" (James 1:27). Rejecting the selfish values of the world, you and I are committed by our relationship with God to *do justice.*

Our study of the Old Testament prophets brings us face-to-face with a dimension of faith that our generation has tended to overlook. The prophets' constant emphasis and God's constant call teach us that today, as well as in ancient Israel, we need to recover a concern for the whole man that God Himself deeply feels.

God calls us today as then to "hate evil, love good, and establish justice in the gate" (Amos 5:15).

SOCIETY/INDIVIDUAL

The Old Testament always portrays reciprocal relationship between the individual and society. Achan's sin (Joshua 7) had its impact on the nation. According to the Law, each individual was made responsible for the suppression of sin in the community, and the dispensing of justice was a community affair. Thus, throughout the Old Testament, the saints at prayer identified themselves with the people around them and confessed, "We have sinned." Habakkuk knew that judgment must fall on Judah and that he himself would not be spared the common experience. Waiting for the day of distress, the prophet trembled . . . but refused to charge God with injustice. Instead, he put his trust in God to bring him, as a trusting individual, through the time of punishment to come.

Accepting responsibility for the condition of Judah, Micah wrote,

> I will bear the indignation of the Lord
> Because I have sinned against Him,
> Until He pleads my case and executes justice
> for me.
>
> *Micah 7:9*

While accepting responsibility with his countrymen for the conditions that led to judgment, Micah

173

at the same time expected justice ultimately to release him.

This points up a delicate balance between the individual's responsibility for society and his personal responsibility to God and to himself. The righteous individual may live in a sinful society and be unable to affect it. But as part of that society, he still bears its burden. He still participates, no matter how unwillingly, in the oppression and injustice around him.

God will vindicate him as an individual for his personal behavior. But God will not free him from discipline for that which is done by the society in which he participates.

Today we tend too often to think "they" do wrong, and because we are not actively involved in doing injustice, we think ourselves free of all taint. But justice is not a passive quality; it is active. Even passive participation in an unjust society makes us share in the responsibility.

INDIVIDUAL RESPONSIBILITY

Along with the above teaching, the Old Testament also makes it clear that each person is responsible for himself.

The prophets Jeremiah and Ezekiel both stressed this fact as the time of Judah's judgment drew near. God would surely discipline His people: the nation would be torn from the land and taken into captivity. *But God would at the same time make distinctions between individuals.* Ezekiel (Ezek. 9) saw angels

174

marking out the men of Jerusalem who had a heart for God so that they might be preserved. In chapter 18, this theme of God's just dealings with individuals is expanded. "If a man is righteous, and practices justice and righteousness," Ezekiel said by the word of the Lord," . . . if he walks in My statutes and My ordinances so as to deal faithfully—he is righteous and will surely live" (18: 5, 9). It may be, the prophet goes on, that a man has a violent son who sheds blood and defrauds his brothers. If this violent son "oppresses the poor and needy, commits robbery, does not restore a pledge, but lifts up his eyes to the idols" (v. 12), he shall not live. But the father is not judged for the sins of the son.

In the same way, a sinful father may have a righteous son. Then the son who "has practiced justice and righteousness, and has observed all My statutes and done them, he shall surely live" (v. 19).

Each individual in the coming national judgment on Judah will live or die for his own sins. And the prophet goes on: a sinner may repent and change his ways. Then he will live. Or a good man may turn to treachery and wickedness. Each will be treated, when the judgment falls, as he is at that time. The sinner will die; the good man will live. And the message concludes with an appeal: " 'Cast away from you all your transgressions which you have committed, and make yourselves a new heart and a new spirit! For why will you die, O house of Israel? For I have no pleasure in the death of anyone who dies,' declares the Lord God. 'Therefore, repent and live' " (vs. 31, 32).

Ezekiel 18 is God's message concerning the life or death of men about to share a judgment announced on the nation. The Captivity will come about as just punishment for the nation's sins. Yet within that national judgment, God will deal fairly and justly with individuals. This passage is *not* dealing with man's eternal condition, and the statement "The soul that sinneth, it shall die" (v. 4, KJV) is not an element of any evangelistic message. It is instead an expression of a basic principle governing God's dealings with men in this world in time of calamity. God is able to distinguish between individuals within the framework of massive tragedy—and does. Individuals are personally responsible, and a commitment to justice and love even within an unjust society (or an unloving church!) is noted and approved by God.

Even if we cannot change the shape of our society, we can act individually in fullest harmony with God's ways.

CONVERSION

This is a final theme that we need to note. Jeremiah and Ezekiel both spoke of a day when God would give the nation Israel a new heart—a heart that would respond to God rather than turn away from Him.

Until the nation knew this conversion, there would be no change in Judah's society.

Centuries later, Nicodemus came to Jesus by night and was astounded by Jesus' teaching that "you must be born again" (John 3:7). Stunned, he asked (perhaps with sarcasm?) how such a thing could be: would a man reenter his mother's womb? Jesus' response is enlightening. "You are a teacher of Israel, and do you not understand these things?" (John 3:10).

The necessity of the new birth was made perfectly clear in the history of Israel as a nation and in the promises of the prophets. Time and time again the nation turned away from a God who loved her. At their first opportunity, the people refused to obey God and enter the Promised Land. This pattern was repeated again and again in Israel and Judah's history, culminating now in the refusal of the people even under severe discipline to respond to God's words to them through Jeremiah. With the perversity of natural man, God's people bridled at His Word and turned rebelliously from His way. As today, the heart of man was untouched by God's love. Only when God acts to give us a new heart are we freed to respond to Him and to find the blessedness of fellowship and fulfillment in Him.

Is conversion necessary?

Look at Israel and Judah. And look at yourself. Apart from personal relationship with God and His action in our lives, we have no hope.

GOING DEEPER

to personalize

1. In this last chapter the author has summed up several "messages" of this time. Select one or two of

the areas he covers, and from the Bible passages covered in this book, either demonstrate the author's point or dispute it.

2. The theme of justice is a dominant one in these prophetic books. From what you have studied in these passages, develop your own definition of justice.

3. Or, write an imaginative prophetic message given by Amos or Micah to the people of your own local church.

4. Or, develop an extended list of opportunities to "do justice" in your own home, church, and community.

Period	Theme	Books
I. PRIMEVAL PERIOD	CREATION Creation to Abraham	*Genesis 1–11* *Job*
II. PATRIARCHAL PERIOD (2166–1446)*	COVENANT Abraham to Moses	*Genesis 12–50*
III. EXODUS PERIOD (1446–1406)	LAW Moses' Leadership	*Exodus* *Numbers* *Leviticus* *Deuteronomy*
IV. CONQUEST OF CANAAN (1406–1390)	CONQUEST Joshua's Leadership	*Joshua*
V. TIME OF JUDGES (1367–1050)	JUDGES No Leadership	*Judges* *Ruth* *I Samuel 1–7*
VI. UNITED KINGDOM (1050–931)	KINGDOM Monarchy Established Establishment (David) Decline (Solomon)	*I Samuel 8–11* *II Samuel 1–24* *I Kings 1–11* *I Chronicles* *II Chronicles* *Psalms* *Ecclesiastes* *Proverbs* *Song of Solomon*

*The dates are taken from *A Survey of Israel's History* by Leon Wood (Grand Rapids: Zondervan, 1975).

VII. DIVIDED KINGDOM (931-586) Israel Elijah Elisha Judah	**PROPHETIC MOVEMENT** Two Kingdoms	*I Kings 12–22* *II Kings 1–17* *II Chronicles 10–29* *Jonah* *Obadiah* *Amos* *Hosea* *Micah* *Joel* *Isaiah*
VIII. SURVIVING KINGDOM (722-586)	Judah Remains	*II Kings 18–25* *II Chronicles 30–36* *Jeremiah* *Nahum* *Zephaniah* *Habakkuk*
IX. BABYLONIAN CAPTIVITY (586-538)	JUDGMENT Torn from Palestine	*Ezekiel* *Daniel* *Esther*
X. RESTORATION (538-400)	The Jews Return *400 Years Between the Testaments*	*Ezra* *Nehemiah* *Haggai* *Zechariah* *Malachi*